DAMNED NEAR KILLED HIM

A chronicle of love, hope and despair in a time of cancer

SANDY GLUM

BIG TREE PUBLISHING
LANGLEY, BC

Published by Big Tree Publishing, Langley, BC Canada
ISBN 978-0-9937030-4-1

Sandy Glum
www.bigtreepublishing.com

Compiled by Sandy Oshiro Rosen
Edited by Lesley Cameron
Designed by Patrice Nelson
Front cover photo by Colourbox

To Anna, Nathan, Bryan
and to the Robinson family,
who lost more than words can express

Contents

Foreword

She still had her long, thick, vibrant red hair when I last spent time with her. Photos of her in the months prior to her passing show her with a shorter, more mature cut and a bit of grey streaking through the red. She was beautiful. Funny, I hardly know where the features of her beauty were most highlighted: in the full smile, in the sparkling eyes and velvety words, or in her laughter, so much laughter ... it never ceased to pour from her lovely lips. Just locking eyes with her would arrest your soul and wrap you in her beauty.

I was not one of the fortunate few who were around her from 2007 to 2010 when the blog entries collected in this book were written. I only knew from friends that she was "struggling with" cancer. I had no idea of how much the disease had progressed until I got word that she had passed. She lived some distance away from me—a ferry ride and a long drive up the coast of Vancouver Island—so we had lost touch over the years.

But I found her again when one of the members of her inner circle—that special group of people who have moved from the realm of friend to family—became a part of my community, bringing with them the grief that time and distance had shielded me from. The pain was made more profound when I discovered her detailed, brutally honest blog. I inhaled her writing in a desperate attempt to rediscover the friend from whom I had been disconnected over the years, trying to grab a tiny thread of her disappearing life before she was lost to me for good.

I found more than I could ever have hoped for. Not only did I find Sandy again, but I also found her young family. Her husband, Bryan, I had known as a smiling, joyful, easygoing young man when they first married, and her grateful reflections on his constant kindness, care, and selflessness while his wife weathered this agony were touching to say the least. Sandy's son, Nathan, was just turning the corner into age eight and her daughter, Anna, was still just four at the time of Sandy's diagnosis. I met them both for the first time in this blog, my heart breaking for them.

The blog was a gift. Not just for its thorough chronicling of the difficulties of daily life for someone who has cancer—the pain, the humiliation, the emotional challenges—but especially for its surprising insights into the mind of Sandy. She was a shy person, but her writing gave her a voice to express her thoughts and feelings that was more insightful than I ever recall making note of. I'm so grateful she chose to entrust us with even the most private of these thoughts.

And she's an accomplished writer, unfolding her experiences as a compelling tale steeped in the curious, the difficult, and the absurd—a tell-all personal account told by a seasoned storyteller.

There are no words to express what spills out from her words into my soul. Her vulnerability both unsettles me and warms my heart. I have combed through this manuscript dozens of times as I have prepared it for printing, and without fail, every time one poignant observation or another has caused me to burst into tears afresh. How can she, in the throes of invasive surgeries, radiation, and chemo, retain her humour while also being so brutally honest about her insecurities, loneliness, anger, disappointment, pain? She reveals a lot to me—about her, about me, about waiting, about suffering. Her words cause me to renegotiate my understanding of "quality of life"—it is not about what we have, but about love ... about who and how we love. Her reflections cause me to appreciate my life, of course, but they also compel me to take stock of how I live. They cause me to recognize the many who silently endure their suffering because they have no means to express it, no attentive friends listening. They challenge me to offer more support to those who are braving chronic illness—there is presumably more to their struggle than most will let on.

The injection of her faith throughout the process is a better theology than we might be able to find at a seminary. She understands that she cannot apply these insights as Band-Aids on a sucking chest wound; they are a balm distilled through the pain of experience, simmered in the heat of confounding realities, and lovingly administered to the broken being.

The title of this book is hers. She used it for her blog, and for those who aren't familiar with the joke, I will tell you Sandy's version. A farmer called the vet one day to come out to his farm and see one of his cows, which was apparently constipated. "He can't poop," said the farmer to the vet, "and I've tried everything. I've walked him around, I've rubbed his stomach, and then I thought I'd try scraping it out. So I shoved a 2x4 up his ass." The vet shook his head in disapproval and said "Rectum." "Wrecked him?" the farmer repeated. "Damned near killed him."

Sandy's diagnosis was rectal cancer, so the title, "damned near killed him" is fitting, not only for the diagnosis but for the humour she found in such ludicrous things. I have kept the blog entries true to the way in which Sandy wrote them, so that we have the privilege of hearing her voice in all its authenticity. Only some names have been changed for privacy reasons.

January 2015
Sandy Oshiro Rosen

2007

September 3, 2007

Life Is Pain, Highness

I have tried in vain, but sleep eludes me. Ignatia has failed me tonight. I think the miasma of unreality is beginning to clear, and the stark truth of my future is beginning to glare at me. I have spilled out the diagnosis to my dearest darlings, and have wept until my eyes are dry and now that I am nothing more than a limp rag, wrung out of all feelings, all thoughts, I begin to see that it is only the beginning. The telling is only the beginning of the pain I will inflict on my friends and family. Now they will watch me sink into sickness and pain, while standing nearby wishing to take it all away and whisk me to safety. "Life is pain, Highness," Wesley says to Buttercup. "Anyone who tells you different is trying to sell you something." But my goal has always been to avoid pain ... to tread carefully lest I hurt someone unknowingly. I'm the one who doles out the tissues, administers the hugs, cooks the meals, tends to the sick. I soothe the pain. I don't inflict it.

And yet here I am. Life is pain, Princess.

I know that hope looms on the horizon, and light can shine in the darkest places ... and all that *but* when I turn out the light, and writhe on my sleepless bed, I'm just tired. And I can't help imagining the horrors to come. And it is only the beginning. And can I be brave enough? Can I? When Lois lay dying from the cancer that ate away her lungs, she said, "I just don't want to be a pansy." I don't want to be a pansy either. A coward. A whiner. I don't want to sap every ounce of strength from my friends, and turn them into blithering idiots who exert all of their internal fortitude bolstering me up, and are left depleted.

I told God that I'm willing to walk down the dark path with Him ... but now I'm not sure. I'm not sure if I can walk down that path bringing all my loved ones along. Psalm 16 begins,

"I love the Lord, for He heard my voice; he heard my cry for mercy. Because He turned His ear to me, I will call on Him as long as I live." Yes. Life *is* pain, *but* the Lord is "gracious and righteous; our God is full of compassion."

I'm the One with a Tumour, I Get to Choose

When asked where we should go for lunch last Sunday, four-year-old Anna paused for a long moment, then said, "Mummy, you're the one with a tumour, you get to choose." It was nice to get to choose something, because in the last few days, my life had changed dramatically and it was suddenly about something momentous that I hadn't chosen at all. My future is defined by something thrust upon me. Cancer. I can say it now, because the biopsy results are back. On Thursday I was feeling almost embarrassed ... that I had created such a furor, and maybe it wasn't cancer at all. I knew within that it was, but hope lingered that it wasn't. But now I know. Yet the unreality of it all still fogs my understanding. I—who always plan in advance and madly organize all aspects of life—am left inept, and utterly unable to plan even a simple birthday party for my son whose eighth birthday is in five days.

And yet, I discover that some choices are still left open. It is ironic that at the very moment when you find that your life is in fact finite, you see endless possibilities. In some crazy way, I realize that with death a more certain certainty than it was last month at this time, I feel a freedom I've never experienced. Freedom to say what I maybe haven't said before, or freedom to let go of what I couldn't release before. Freedom to speak of my faith as if it is as real as I've always known it is in my heart. Freedom to be alive. Alive in a very quiet way—it is still me, after all. No hot air balloon rides, or skydiving expeditions. Maybe I'll write more, hug my kids more, tell my family how much I love them, refuse to be irritated by socks discarded on the floor. Maybe.

And maybe great things will happen. Freedom does that, I think.

September 14, 2007

On Tuesday

On Tuesday I entered a building I had never imagined would have anything to do with me. An unassuming building, fairly institutional but with obvious effort at good taste and soothing decor. As I wandered almost flippantly through the front door, I glanced through the doorway of a room entitled "Quiet Room." Plush couches dominated the room, but scattered about were boxes of tissue. It was those damn tissues that got to me. My thin veneer of lightheartedness vanished, and I began to quake.

I'm glad Laurie was there to hold my hand and help me find the right office. Up and down the stairs three times before we figured out where "Lab B" was. "Lab B." Now there's an inspirational name for you. "Lab B" at the BC Cancer Clinic. Has a nice ring to it.

Eventually I met the radiation oncologist who will oversee my treatment, a thin, quiet-spoken man who seemed to stutter over the word, "cancer" and who was very apologetic about the various indignities he had to visit upon my body. I read somewhere that people should always whistle while they work, but I was grateful that Dr. A. seemed unaware of the maxim.

He told me that radiation would kill my ovaries and launch me into early menopause. Nice. Hot flashes, irritability, and mood swings as well as stitches, catheters and a reconstructed rectum.

I like my ovaries. I've grown accustomed to them. The thought of losing them sent funny feelings dancing through my tummy, and I'm afraid I didn't really hear much more of the doctor's carefully worded advice.

Ridiculous, really. I have cancer, for cryin' out loud—I don't have time to worry about a few eggs and a future of estrogen depletion. And yet, I find the prospect strangely upsetting.

Maybe it was the dawning realization of all the losses I will face. All the repercussions. I dunno. Of course I will do the therapy if I need to. I'm determined to do what I need to do to survive.

We celebrated my son's eighth birthday today. A sweet freckle-faced boy with too many teeth in his enormous grin and a delightfully gurgling laugh. It was a happy day, with friends, family, good food, and presents. A day of memories and laughter ... and a shadow ... and a lingering fear.

September 29, 2007

I Am Undone

Four weeks ago today, I got my diagnosis. In some ways it seems like only days ago, and in other ways it seems a lifetime away. How can one person experience so many emotions in four short weeks? Sometimes I worry that the top of my head is going to blow off. To my relief, I no longer feel as though I am about to shake off these mortal coils any time soon. And yet. Cancer is still a pretty powerful word, as words go.

Really, I think I am almost numb. With so many raging emotions racing through my body, I am left rather limp and ragged. Yesterday, the school accountant told Bryan that someone had paid our children's tuition for the entire year. That's four thousand dollars. Four. Thousand. Dollars.

No words exist to express my heart. I am undone. All I can do is weep.

I remember a little how I felt when I first realized that Jesus's sacrifice was for me, too. Unworthy. Paltry. But loved ... with such a love I didn't know existed. With no way to repay ... and no need to repay. With no words to say ... and no words needed. Undone in the face of such benevolence and goodness. Such lavish generosity.

I felt a little of that yesterday. I have done nothing to deserve such a gift. Helplessly grateful and silent, I accept.

I told Tony that I have trouble receiving. And that I knew I would have to learn how to receive the gifts people wanted to give. But I didn't know how excruciatingly difficult it would be. How broken and helpless I would feel. How powerless.

Chris talks about self as an idol that we must cast down. I cast it down. Or, at least I try. Is this what it's all about? Or is it about anything at all?

It's All About Me

One of the most peculiar things about this past month was how time continued to march inexorably on. Mundane tasks and appointments nipped at my heels: lunches, piano lessons, dance class ... and the crowning insult of all, mounds and mounds of laundry. Surely time should stop, suspended by the tragedy of a serious disease? Surely life should become embalmed, preserved from the buffets of minutiae. Surely one should be exempt from laundry.

And yet, I find myself grateful for these tasks that remind me that I am still here, and that life does go on. One of the most trying things about being ill is that people tend to think they need to protect you from unpleasantness. Thinking you have enough to worry you, they exclude you from their own trials and difficulties, with the inevitable result that you feel more alone than before. More crippled. More useless.

I'm the person I was five weeks ago, just refined a little by sorrow and care. I worry that this friend seems depressed or that the other is experiencing difficulties with her pregnancy, and I want to be a part of these concerns. But sometimes I'm not allowed in. And sometimes my head is too full to hear. I am distracted by my body, and I fret that all I talk about is my body. I worry that I am boring everyone with repeated discussions about appointments, plans, procedures, and speculations. I don't want to lose my ability to laugh, or to see the utter absurdities of life, or to share in the sorrows of others. But there is a sense of self-absorption that is really appalling. To some degree, everything *is* about me.

I think I'm a little depressed tonight. I probably shouldn't write late at night when the rain is pelting with unwonted ferocity at my window. I think I'll go wrap myself in my luxurious new blankie and listen to Pavarotti until my mind relaxes and I can sleep.

October 6, 2007

The Madwoman in the Attic

Tony asked me today how I am feeling about the surgery. I only grinned at him in a very foolish way. How can I say it without sounding cheesy, or insincere, or delusional? I feel great! Sort of giddy and excited. Buoyant. Happy. Glad to be moving forward. Ten days ago, when I first realized that surgery was imminent, I felt a clutch of fear around my heart. I lost my breath. I lost my focus. I couldn't sit still, and wandered about my house like a demented banshee, wailing and wringing my hands.

And then I had an epiphany. I stopped dead in the tracks of my looming hysteria, and asked myself, "What are you afraid of?" After a moment of pondering, I had no answer. I tried tracing back my thoughts to see if I could discover what had brought on such a strong and fearful reaction, but I couldn't find it. So I realized that I had been chasing phantoms. I have nothing to fear.

That is a hugely profound statement for me. I have been plagued by fear, defined by fear, "cabin'd, cribbed, confined" by fear all my life. The irony is not lost on me. The moment when some would say I have a legitimate reason to fear, is the moment when I am freed from it. The moment when dread, confusion and darkness should threaten me is the moment I achieve clarity and light. It's a mystery.

I just hope I haven't peaked too soon. I have a lot of hours to pass before Tuesday 0645.

October 9, 2007

A Birth Day

The house is eerily quiet tonight. I've never been in my house at night without my children sleeping nearby. I wouldn't have thought the sound of two small sleeping bodies would make such a difference, but it does. Tonight my children sleep at Laurie's, and I know they sleep secure and happy.

I have to be at the hospital very early in the morning, and I should be sleeping, but my mind is too unquiet for sleep. I don't feel worried or anxious. Maybe restless. I can't seem to settle to any task. My belongings are scattered across the room, and my bag gapes emptily at me.

Five years ago tonight, I also wandered my house restlessly. My labour pains had intensified, and I knew that my baby would be born. At 2:04 a.m. she arrived—a beautiful, round, black-haired baby girl with eyes the colour of a stormy sea. My Anna.

What I remember most about that moment is her eyes. So steady and unwavering. She didn't blink at all, just gazed at me. My heart. I thought maybe it would stop beating, it was so full. It didn't stop, but from that moment it was held captive by my sweet, impetuous, imperious little dancing princess.

Saying goodbye to Anna and Nathan last night was painful. I wanted to clutch them to me greedily. I wanted to weep over them and avow my love over and over, but I knew that would do nothing but churn everyone up and ruin any possibility of sleep. So, I just snuggled them gently, said "I love you" once, and let them go.

There's that phrase again "Let go."

I'm not a let-goer. I'm a hold-oner. A cling-on-er.

But tomorrow morning I have to let everything go. Everything. I hope I can do it with grace and courage. I hope I can do it with laughter. I hope I can do it.

October 21, 2007

Sunday Oct 14 – 5 Days Post Op

My life is constantly descending into absurdities. Diagnosed with rectal cancer, given an anterior resection of the rectum, four-day epidural, plunging heart rate and blood pressure, and a seven-inch scar on my abdomen. And what is it that brings me to tears? Urinating.

I wonder why it is that the simplest biological functions cause me such grief? Getting pregnant was excruciatingly difficult. What most women can accomplish in one good romp in the hay took me ten years to accomplish. And now urinating—the most basic human function seems elusive and impossible. So now I lay in bed, absorbing the most serene and relaxing music; I close my eyes, think of rain, and wait.

I wonder, briefly, if Jesus ever had trouble peeing. The Bible says that He is intimately acquainted with all human suffering. Before I entered the hospital, I thought a lot about Jesus, and His familiarity with pain and suffering. I pictured Him hungry, exhausted, sleep deprived, homeless. I saw Him relinquish His desire for wife, family, home. Alone, lonely, betrayed, tortured. I saw Him gasping for His last breath as He hung dying on the cross. I knew that there wasn't anything about suffering that He didn't already know.

But I forgot to imagine Him having trouble peeing.

To help me prepare to be brave and serene in this ordeal, I imagined myself many times welcoming people to my sick bed sporting a brave and patient smile on my face.

I didn't see myself weeping hysterically, shaking uncontrollably over my inability to void my bladder. How did I get here?

I loathe what this is doing to Bryan. Today he looked wild-eyed and defeated. He is exhausted and worried and stretched by too many responsibilities. I've tried so hard not to be too demanding, but I've been frightened and lonely; I've had too many bad nights.

I'm sucking the life out of Laurie.

I hate what this is doing to me. What it is turning me into. I'm so needy. So weepy. So weak.

Somehow I can trust Jesus in the big stuff, but I can't seem to manage it in the little stuff. I'm horribly inconsistent.

How will we manage if this journey is longer that we thought it would be? How will I protect my loved ones from being sucked into the abyss with me?

Don't have any answers today.

Later.

When presented with the question of Jesus having trouble peeing, Fergie said emphatically, "Of course he did! When He wandered in the desert for forty days."

A lightning bolt of truth from a twelve-year-old. How unutterably beautiful and profound this strange day has been. Tumultuous and tiring. Sad and still. Quiet and reflective. Ridiculous and enlightening.

And Laurie is pouring herself into me because she loves me. She loves me and she delights in caring for me with tenderness and ferocity. It is what love does. It is right and good. And it is what I would do for her. Her presence in my life now is such a source of light and hope to me. When she enters the room, she brings with her such a presence of wisdom, competence and understanding that my embattled spirit finds rest and ease. Fear lightens and I can breathe again. I think what I'm learning most is that true friendship doesn't speak about debt, it just accepts the gifts that are offered with love.

I am being stripped bare.

October 21, 2007

Monday, Oct 15

I know I'm a neophyte in this cancer business, but in my short experience, I've been awed by the tumultuous vat of emotion stirred up by the word. Everyone has a story. Everyone has a certain degree of terror. And it's odd how the word seems to give people a license to speak—to speak freely and sometimes fiercely about the disease, about their fears, about friends and family who have suffered.

My first nurse in ICU was visibly shaken when he spoke of his terror. "One in two people get it, you know," he whispered hoarsely. "I know it's going to get me." And when he spoke of me to other nurses, he always referred to me as, "One of the lucky ones."

I may be over-sensitive, but I found that a little nerve-racking in the hours immediately following my surgery.

Everyone has wanted to know how it was detected in the first place. I began to feel that my story was a strange one indeed—but why it was strange, I was never able to puzzle out. Is it because of my age? "You're too young to have this," has been the universal refrain. Is it because the surgeon seemed to "get it all"? I don't know.

I don't think I have really acquiesced to the certainty of cancer yet. After I had experienced a particularly difficult night, I was feeling limp and shaky. When the day nurse came on duty, he asked (in the forced-jolly voice nurses like to use), "So, what do you think of abdominal surgery so far?" I said, "Not a big fan." When I said that I thought I was a bit depressed, he said, "Do you think that might have something to do with the fact that you have just had a huge surgery, and that you have cancer?"

I was a little taken aback. He said it so casually, so matter-of-factly. I think I had forgotten that I had cancer. I was concentrating so hard on the surgery, I forgot the reason why the surgery was necessary in the first place.

A couple of nights ago, when I was feeling sad and bereft again, another nurse spoke of her fears. Her daughter's latest pap test had shown some irregularities, and the mom was clearly terrified. I had been struggling all day to remain positive, and not let my fears command my thoughts, but fear had run rampant in her, and she could not contain herself. She kept imagining the "what if's," the worst case scenarios. What about her daughter's new baby growing up without a mummy? First steps, first day of school, graduation day, wedding day? My thoughts had been there many times before, and I was trying not to let them scatter in that direction again. "Be positive," people say. But they invariably follow this injunction with a sad or fearful thought we would not want to dwell on.

Then my latest nurse. In the witching hour last night, she began ever so tentatively to ask me about my cancer. How was it detected? Why did I seek medical help in the first place? I knew that something lurked behind her questions. And soon she was speaking of her son. He had cancer. And he had been very sick. She spoke for a long time in a quiet whisper, and became very emotional. When she was done, I said, "Thank you." She shook her head and said with tears, "No, thank you." And she hugged me.

But I don't know why. Why did she thank me?

I have so many miles to go.

October 22, 2007

A Week Later

I wrote this post and the previous two longhand while I was in hospital. Maybe by tomorrow, I'll be up to date.

Tuesday, Oct 16

A week since the surgery. And what a week. Trepidation and exultation. Pain and relief. Tears and laughter. And love. So much love. So much kindness, tenderness and care.

I remember sitting on the operating table waiting for the epidural to be inserted. It was just before 8:00 a.m. and the doctors and nurses were just beginning their day. There was the early-morning start-of-work quiet anticipation and bustle as everything was made ready. I was trying to remain calm and focussed, but I kept hearing a strange clinking sound that disturbed my calm. I glanced around to identify the sound. It was a nurse standing around a long table, moving some shiny things. As my eyes focussed, I realized that she was organizing surgical instruments.

"Oh," I thought, "those are for cutting ... me." My heart plunged into the icy well of fear. With shallow breaths, I recited the verse I had chosen as my hospital verse: "The Lord God is with you. He is mighty to save ..." over and over.

I thought it prudent to keep my eyes closed and pray. I really didn't want to see anything else.

I heard the anesthetist say "Oops" as he put the IV needle in my arm, and I opened my eyes to see a long spurt of blood across the white blanket that covered my legs. "That's my blood," I thought in a detached sort of way. I said, "'Oops' is not a word that should be used in the OR." And I resolved to *keep* my eyes closed.

Within moments, I was ready, and the anesthetic took over.

Next I knew, I was being wheeled out to the recovery room. I was disoriented, and struggled to come into myself again. My mouth was so dry and I felt like I was suffocating. Dr. B. came to check on me.

"She's a good patient," said a nurse.

"She *is* a good patient," he replied. I felt quite proud of myself. Everything was vague and dream-like. Time had no meaning. I felt restless, anxious. I needed to see the faces of people who loved me.

When it came time to move me upstairs, Bryan, Laurie and Shannon were there to meet me. They smiled, cried a little bit and held my hands. I rested, finally, buoyed by their loving, strong, thankful spirits.

Dr. B. stopped by and said, "You must have had all those school children praying for you in mass assembly."

"I did!" I said.

"Well, you obviously had someone up there doing battle for you today."

"I did, I did," I whispered.

And I knew it was true. The power of God was so real to me in that room, I didn't know why everyone couldn't feel it. It was thick, palpable. Soothing. Electric. I floated on it as on a vast blue ocean bathed in light.

At one point, I remember thinking, "There's almost too much power here. I have all I need." So I asked God to send some of that strong healing power around to others. To my friends' unborn baby. To the man groaning with pain in the next bed.

Even in the night, when it was dark, and my body was doing

scary things, I knew God was there. He held me in the darkness and uncertainty.

What do I remember most about that day?

I remember the kindnesses of strangers. The OR nurse who held my hands and wiped away my tears. The ICU nurse who washed me and settled me in bed for the night.

Those who came in the darkness to care for a body that was out of control.

I remember Shannon sitting by my bed, knitting. How unutterably comforting was the gentle clicking of her needles. I remember her smile—so loving, so gentle.

I remember Laurie standing by my bed, looking down at me and loving me.

I remember the relief in Bryan's eyes.

I remember feeling loved and safe, happy and content, relieved and exhausted. I remember that every time I opened my eyes, someone who loved me was there to smile at me and help me know I was going to be all right.

October 24, 2007

My Flesh and My Heart May Fail

Last Monday (Oct. 15th) I came home from hospital. I was supposed to stay one more night, but they needed my bed. I could have spent the night in a holding tank in Emerg, or I could have had the weeny little alcove in the hallway; fortunately my surgeon was still in the building, and he gave permission for me to go home. I was incandescent with happiness.

Besides the malfunctioning plumbing inside my body, my recovery has been fantastic. By the fifth day post op. I was able to get out of bed easily, and roam the hallways at will. Every time my surgeon came to my bedside, he marveled at how well I looked.

Another surgeon I know slightly happened to come to my room looking for someone else. When he saw me, he said, "You've had your surgery? You don't *look* like you've been hit by a truck. That's how people usually look after that surgery!" I felt special.

I attribute my remarkable recovery to three factors:

1. The power of God

2. The intervention of my-friend-the-witch-doctor (aka Tony, the Homeopath—God bless him)

3. A kick-ass epidural—almost entirely pain-free for three days!

A remarkable recovery, but not without setbacks. By Thursday morning, I was huddled in Emerg with a drastically malfunctioning bladder. *Arghh!*

Dr. B. had urged me to come in so he could look at me and help me. When I arrived, I was in a lot of pain and feeling so desperately tired of it all. But a crusty old nurse with two artificial knees and an abdominal scar wider than Saskatchewan put a weak smile on my face with her blunt observations and advice.

"You don't want to spend any more time in here, Honey. When I had my knees replaced, I wouldn't let any of 'em touch me. I just told 'em to leave the stuff at the door, and I'd do everything myself." Comforting words indeed.

She put me in a private room—little more than a broom closet, really. "You need some privacy—nothin' worse than not being able to pee."

I agreed fervently.

Soon Dr. B. arrived. The world is a crazy place when the arrival of a relative stranger can make your heart lift so. He stood across the room as a nurse prepared to rub my lower belly with an ultrasound thinger to measure the amount of urine in my bladder. I winced as she gingerly tore off the steri-strips.

"I've had your pathology report back," Dr. B. said conversationally.

I tried to focus on his face, but the Ativan tablet ("the equivalent of a three drink buzz, Honey") was wreaking havoc with my concentration.

"It says that there is lymph node involvement."

I gazed at him blankly. What? Why was he standing across the room telling me this? Why wasn't he standing beside my bed, grasping my hand reassuringly? Why was he telling me this now? Was he attempting to distract me from my bladder, and the indignities being performed on my body?

My eyes filled with tears, and my traitorous lower lip trembled.

"We removed 36 lymph nodes, and 18 of them were involved. This means you *will* have to have further treatment. Radiation or chemo. Or both."

I heard his voice only faintly. He seemed a hundred miles away. Surely he wasn't speaking to me. I was done. The cancer was removed. I was done.

I couldn't stem the flow. I looked away and gritted my teeth.

I remember feeling so annoyed that he was across the room. I think he was trying to give me some privacy while the nurse fiddled with my bladder. But the truth is, I have cancer and there is no such thing as privacy for me anymore.

Later, when the bladder crisis was over, and I was in my right mind again, he did come to my side and grip my hand with a healing touch. I felt better. A bit.

But it doesn't change the fact that I have to go to the Cancer Clinic again. I have to take the Cancer Van to the Cancer Clinic and stay at the Cancer Lodge. For weeks, maybe.

That's a little hard to take.

I think I had spent so much time thinking about the surgery, so much energy concentrating on being positive and hopeful about the surgery and the recovery that I had fooled myself into thinking that was the end of it all. I think it's okay to be a bit disappointed about that. I would rail against my fate, but I'm not really a railer. I'll probably ooze a few tears.

It's funny in a way. A month ago, when I first went to the Cancer Clinic and heard about the possibility of weeks of treatments in Victoria, I remember thinking, "I can't do that. I'll never be able to do that."

And yet, it transpires that I can do that. I can do that. It will be miserable and inconvenient, and horribly disruptive to my children ... but I can do that. What else can I do?

Here's what I read today, "My flesh and my heart may fail, but God is the strength of my heart and my portion forever." Ps 73:26

Yep. Big sigh. I'm going to be okay.

October 25, 2007

A Jar of Clay

The sun is shining today through the crisp autumn air, and frost is glinting on the grass in my backyard. It's the kind of day I would normally greet with a flash of fierce happiness. Autumn is my favourite season; sunshine on a frosty garden, my favourite sight. The strange thing about my life right now is that I am so at the mercy of my healing body that I feel utter detachment from almost everything else. For that matter, I even feel detached from my body. When I look down at the thin scarlet thread on my abdomen, I feel a surreal disconnection—that's not my body. When I rub my palm across the scar, and feel only a weird numbness and a vague itch, I wonder whose body this is.

Yesterday I had a bad day. People keep saying, "You'll have some good days and some bad days." But that doesn't help. I don't like bad days. They make me feel petulant and unhappy, immature, ungrateful and crabby. Tears lurk around every sad song I listen to on my iPod—and on bad days, I listen to a lot of sad songs.

It's just that my body is so vulnerable, so sensitive to every nuance of change; each new food I try, each new drink I introduce, each bit of fabric that rubs the wound seems to send my body into a tailspin of catching up and adjusting. I know I sound whiny. And crabby. And petulant. But there it is.

Today my tummy is better, so I can look at the day with a bit more equanimity. We may try to go out for dinner tonight. My mom has been trapped in my house for two weeks, and is in need of some time out; I need to feel normal; my kids need some fun and Bryan needs a break. It's a good thing it's me that's sick—I would not be nearly as patient and accommodating as Bryan is.

Enough. Today I will look at the sun, I will walk around the block, I will enjoy the company of friends and family and I will eat a good supper. I think if I could get my appetite back, and lose this constant queasiness, I would be more hopeful. Good digestion goes a long way toward mental and emotional well-being.

I'm a little afraid of what chemo is going to do to this fragile shell that houses me. This jar of clay is easily broken.

October 27, 2007

Jar of Clay Part Two: The Treasure Bit

So yesterday, I felt fragile and broken: a jar of clay riddled with fissures and flaws. I napped, I rested and I waited ... for my bowels to start working again. I tire of my bowels.

It was a blue, melancholy day—a day in which I wondered if I would be able to attain the heights of optimism I had reached just before my surgery, when I felt empowered, expectant, excited, enthralled. Ready.

I know that if I am to battle my way to health and strength, I need to feel positive and optimistic. But some days it's hard.

I managed to summon the energy to go out for dinner, but I was fading fast by the time we returned home. My wound hurt, I was nauseous and discouraged.

Then as we were entering the house, we noticed a white package tucked under the shutter; we pried it loose and went inside. We opened it to find $300 worth of Overwaitea gift cards. Randy had brought them by and had left a sweet note. I burst into tears, and cried for half an hour.

Why is it that when you don't think you can take any more, God gives you more? I crumbled under the weight of such continuous kindness and generosity. Last night I felt broken. I am a jar of clay, ready to crumble to dust at the least provocation.

Yes, I am a jar of clay, fragile and vulnerable, *but* that is irrelevant. What's important here is that this vessel contains a treasure, an "all surpassing power [that] is from God and not from [me.]" I am "hard pressed on every side, but not crushed; perplexed, but not in despair; persecuted, but not abandoned; struck down, but not destroyed."

I know I've been crabby and sad, disappointed and scared, lonely and worried. But through it I have felt the presence of God. I've known His power in the still, quiet places in my heart. It's been the cleft in the rock where I have hid through these minor storms that have buffeted me.

A couple of times, I have thought that this is a dark road to travel. But what I've begun to see is that no place is too dark, when I carry the light of Jesus with me.

For God, who said, "Let light shine out of darkness," made his light shine in our hearts to give us the light of the knowledge of the glory of God in the face of Christ.

October 30, 2007

Life in the Gap

I've been contemplating the possibility, or rather the inevitability, of picking up the threads of my regular life, and I admit that I find the prospect a bit daunting. During the last three weeks I've been in a strange cocoon where minutes melt into hours, and hours into days with no responsibilities or duties—nothing but time to while away in reading, listening to music, thinking—lots and lots of thinking. I can't recall any other period in my life characterized by such leisure and such lassitude. Some days I've barely been able to hold a book, much less read it. And TV? Nope. I would have thought I'd be glued to the set in weary boredom and a longing to pass the time. But I've found the idea of TV really tasteless. No TVs were allowed in ICU, and then when I moved to the regular ward, I had no desire to be entertained. I had experienced such a rarified atmosphere in ICU, I didn't want to profane it with TV. Sounds pretty highfaluting, as my mom would say, but what it really means is that I had done some thinking, and praying, some listening and reading and I had a lot of thoughts floating around. Some I pursued, and some I let slip away for now.

I can't explain it any better than to say that I needed time to *be* in the moment, and not avoid the moment. I'm a past master at avoiding the moment, but I wanted this time to be more than three weary weeks of filling time. I wanted more.

I'm still thinking, but an idea that keeps popping up is the idea of letting go. I like the word "relinquish" even though it's a pretty general word. It can mean simply "releasing one's hold on something," or the more complicated "reluctantly giving up control." I like both meanings; they each have a different nuance. I've spoken before about my inability to let go. I'm like the proverbial dog which returns to its own vomit. I don't like returning to the messes I've made, but many times I just can't help myself. Sometimes I return in the hopes that I can fix things, clean up the mess, or better yet prevent the mess in the first place. I stew and stew about the same things. I strangle my thoughts with "what ifs" and "yeah buts." But it's not just my thoughts I cling to. I want to control my circumstances. I've never been very flexible—never really able to abandon expectations and just accept life as it happens. I'm better at it now than I was ten years ago—having children necessitates a certain measure of flexibility, a willingness to suspend or even utterly abandon carefully designed plans. But I have a long way to go.

I want my life to go my way. I talk about wanting to yield to God, to follow the Holy Spirit, to walk in His will; but I still want life to go my way. Very arrogant, I know. And I know that there have been clear moments in my life when I have yielded very nicely to God, usually after a tremendous struggle and an ocean of tears. So I know it is possible.

When I was thinking about speaking at grad, I suddenly thought, "I hope I have hair." It worried me for a few minutes. And then I thought, "Can I abandon that hope?" I guess I can. It would probably be good for me to be bald. I would save so much time.

I know I'll come back to this idea again and again in the coming months—it seems to be the constant refrain of my life. Give up. Surrender. Yield. Waive. Abandon.

And so, when I contemplate returning to my life, I feel a bit tremulous inside. On the weekend, I did three things that represent normalcy for me: I went out for tea with a friend, I went to church, and I tutored. Each event caused a minor stir. Tea felt really strange; I'm not really an invalid at this point, and yet I felt sort of weak and pallid. I struggled with conversation; I struggled with my tea; I struggled with how to do this ritual. At church I panicked whenever someone approached me. What should I say? How should I act? How could I still be me after everything that had happened to me, and in me? Lots of things are happening *to* me without my permission, and even more things are happening because I am active in this whole process. I'm learning to yield, to cease my endless striving and to know God. But returning to life is a bit of a danger. Will I forget? Will I take up my own cause again? Or will I remember what happened in the cocoon?

October 31, 2007

Pack Up Your Troubles

I can't shake off this pervading air of sadness. Last night I decided to go to my dance class: the final class in the session I had begun before the surgery. I thought it would be fun. I thought it would be nice to watch my friends dance, and to remind myself that life goes on, that the dance goes on and that one day I will join in the dance again. I thought it would be a good reminder of the power, and the strength and the grace that once were mine. I wasn't prepared for the utter desolation that swept over me. The sense of loss.

As I watched the swirling skirts and the undulating figures, I was sort of devastated by the thought of what I was missing out on—both now, and in the near future. No pumpkin carving for Halloween. No swinging up my daughter and catching her in my arms. No Christmas concert. No shopping for stocking stuffers. No dancing. I know it was completely futile. Useless. Unhelpful. Stupid.

But I couldn't help myself. I've been reading a book called *When the Body Says No*. It examines the role of stress and emotional repression in the development of disease and sickness; a very interesting book, but a bit depressing. Everyone dies. They lose their hair, they are crippled with pain, they never claw their way out of emotional turmoil ... and they die. It's sad.

And then, people are always telling me about people who have died from cancer. And who have been devastated by the effects of chemotherapy. And I wonder to myself, "In what way do you imagine this to be helpful to me?" I'm straining with everything in me not to think about dying.

But, of course I can't help my mind from wandering in that direction. Death lurks behind every dark place in my thoughts.

I really don't think I'm on the verge of death. Now. But I can't help wondering about the future—what kind of respite have I won here, anyway?

And I keep trying to be normal. But last night on the way home from dance, I burst into tears and wailed hysterically, "But I can't be normal, I can't! Nothing about this is normal!" And I can't see far enough into the future to see when anything will be normal ever again.

Hence the melancholy.

I keep telling people that I'm doing well. I smile. I talk about the incredible mercies and provisions of God. I emphasize the good I've seen, and the hope I have. And all this is true. It is.

How can a person feel so many opposing emotions at the same time—how can a person have hope and despair at the same time? Peace and fear? Rest and restlessness? Joy and sorrow? I don't know how. I don't want to pack away all those hard, sad feeling into a bag and push them under the bed. I want to hang them up like garments and look at them. I want to iron out the wrinkles, run my hands over the fabric and examine them. And then I want to fold them up and send them off to the thrift store. Maybe someone else can use them.

November 8, 2007

The Power of Negative Thinking

I've been thinking a lot over the past week. Some of those thoughts have been fairly lachrymose, and I've wondered if I'm slipping into a funk. But, I've come to realize that sadness is part of the deal right now. Positive thinking is all very well, and it has buoyed me up wonderfully over the last eight weeks, but there is a place for the power of negative thinking. Not negative as in pessimistic, or fatalistic; but negative in the sense of looking honestly at my situation and evaluating what is working, what is not working, and what to do about it. A willingness to look at the hard things sometimes leads to acceptance, and acceptance can lead to healing. I'm not talking about the healing of my cancer, but rather the healing of this wretched sense of woundedness that pervades my being. I do feel that I'm wounded and bleeding in places that no one can see—places that I can barely see myself.

I was looking on the Canadian Cancer Society website, looking for information on chemotherapy and radiation. I crave knowledge, as if knowledge is some sort of insulation against pain. After being thoroughly discouraged by descriptions of vomiting, ruined bowels, hair loss, premature menopause and other assorted goodies, I switched to so-called inspirational stories of survival. I think my hair is still standing on end. I looked for people who had survived colorectal cancer, and found a woman who had been diagnosed in 1995. "That sounds promising," I naively thought. *Eeeeesh!* Yes, she survived the colorectal cancer (which was surgically removed) and the subsequent rounds of radiation and chemo—*but* the cancer showed up in her breast a few years later, then in her right lung (which was completely removed) and then later in her left lung! *Argh!* I'm afraid I rate this pretty low on the scale of inspirational "survival" stories. And the next few stories were just as appalling.

So there you have it. I had been wondering if my thoughts over the last week or so had been too despondent. Up until last week, I had never entertained the thought of the cancer recurring. But last week I started looking a little more honestly at my situation. When the tumour was removed, I rather foolishly thought I was done with cancer. Then when the pathology report showed lymph node involvement, I reluctantly accepted that I wasn't finished. Still, I clung to the hope that I soon would be finished—maybe by Christmas, it would all be behind me. However, after talking with a friend who has recently dealt with breast cancer, I see that this may be a vain hope. Radiation may take several weeks, and chemo will probably follow that, and not run concurrently as I had imagined. And the more I look at my life from this moment on, the more I see cancer—or the possibility of cancer. Therein lies my sense of woundedness and loss.

My "deepest truth" (as Gabor Maté calls it) is that I am hurt, sad and frightened. Not "a little" or "a bit"—but deeply, profoundly, abidingly. And yet, looking at this truth unflinchingly gives a sense of freedom and empowerment. There is nothing to lose in truth ... except maybe fear of the unknown.

Maté says that acceptance is "simply the willingness to recognize and accept how things are. It is the courage to permit negative thinking to inform our understanding, without allowing it to define our approach to the future." So, I need to have the courage to accept my reality, without allowing it to define my future. I mean, it will obviously define some things about my future. I will always have to have cancer screening and be vigilant about my health; and this will be a huge adjustment for a person who up until eight weeks ago visited the doctor rarely and with great unwillingness. But it doesn't have to define my feelings about my life or my future. It doesn't have to leave me feeling like a damp rag wrung with grief.

I know that a lot of what I've said about my immediate future is purely speculative. I really won't know anything until tomorrow, when I see the oncologists in Victoria. But in a weird way, it has helped me to look at my future in terms of the worst, so that maybe I'll be pleasantly surprised by the best—or at least prepared for the reality.

And maybe I'll get lunch at The Blethering Place.

November 10, 2007

Dust in the Wind

Pretty exhausted today. Yesterday I had some appointments at the Cancer Clinic in Victoria, and by the end of my visit, I was reeling with an overload of information, grief, desperation and relief.

"We consider you cured," said the medical oncologist.

"Oh," I replied, a little confused. I wondered why I had just driven 3 hours in the darkness and rain.

"Yes, cured. But now you need a little insurance—6 months' worth."

"Six months?" I faltered.

Yes. Six months. Five weeks of radiation and low doses of chemo. Five weeks in Victoria away from my family. Five weeks of living alone among strangers. Five weeks of sleeping uneasily in a room with a stranger, talking awkwardly with fellow lodgemates over jigsaw puzzles, eating cafeteria food, and watching my body crumble under the effects of radiation.

But wait—there's more. This is followed by fifteen weeks of chemotherapy in Campbell River. Fifteen weeks of mouth sores, skin rashes, diarrhea, nausea, itchy palms and sore feet.

But ...

They consider me cured. What a lovely word. Let me take a moment to roll it on my tongue. Savour it. It comes from the Latin "curare," which means "take care of." Yes. I have been taken care of, and I will be taken care of in the next six months; I know it.

But I still couldn't help a few desperate tears this morning. You know when you deliberately look at the worst case scenario, while all the time secretly hope and frantically wish for the best?

So, I cried. And all the time I cried, I felt little fingers of guilt tickle the back of my neck. How could I cry, and be so sad when God had been so good; when He had cured me in every sense of the word, and provided for all my needs? I kept thinking that I shouldn't feel like this, I shouldn't; but, I couldn't help it.

And then I read Psalm 103:13–14. "As a father has compassion on his children, so the Lord has compassion on those who fear him; for he knows how we are formed, he remembers that we are dust."

He remembers, as I so often do not, that I am made of dust. So fine and dry and powdery that the wind can scatter me in any direction. So weak and formless that I have no substance. And yet, He has compassion on me, like the father He is. I must break His heart, and yet He runs with open arms to welcome me when I turn. He knows that I feel sad, and He mourns over me, as Bryan mourns over Anna when her heart seems broken. He knows, as she so often doesn't, that the earthshaking trage- dy breaking her heart is no more than a passing shadow. A light and momentary trouble.

I will rally. I must.

November 14, 2007

A Living Hope

A couple of days ago I was reading the blog of a young woman who had been diagnosed with a rare and inoperable cancer. She said that the one thing she didn't want was to be changed; she didn't want the cancer to change who she is. Those words sort of settled into my consciousness for days. I think I understand some of what she meant—I've been struggling for weeks to find the essential me in all the craziness that has been happening in my body and to my body. "I'm still me!" I've shouted in the silence.

But at the same time, I want to change. Somehow in this scourging of my body, I want to experience a corresponding scourging of my spirit. Wait. "Want" might be too strong a word; it might imply more acquiescence and less reluctance than I really feel. Still, I know there is a stirring in my soul that longs for higher things, and this seems like the time to search them out. It seems necessary to have a thinning of the curtain between this world and the next before I am able take stock and consider myself aright. I've had glimpses before—when a loved one has died, or faced a danger averted. But for real change to occur, there has to be more proximity. More urgency.

I was reading a homily on healing the other day. It said that in order to receive the "action of the grace of God unto healing of body or soul, or of both—we must open ourselves to God. Not to healing, but to God." And I remembered that some time in the summer I had prayed "I am willing, Lord. Take me where ever you need me to go." I want to change. I want to be open to God, as frightening and soul flaying as that might be. Because being open to God means being open to the scrutiny of the One. I know that nothing is hidden from Him, but there is a difference in God seeing all, and deliberately opening ourselves to His all-seeing-ness. There's an awful lot I don't really want to reveal.

The homily goes on to suggest that we seek healing because we want to forget that our bodies are mortal, that our own powers cannot restore us to health, that we will deteriorate and fade away. But perhaps a reminder of our mortality is a good thing. Perhaps it will help us to "shake off everything that is fatal to us." Not just fatal to our bodily health, but worse, what is fatal to our spiritual health. What kills the life of the spirit within us? What prevents us from living the eternal life that is ours to live now, in the present?

To be healed does not mean to become well so that I can go back to the life I lived before; it means to be well so that I can begin life anew. Perhaps the illness is like the old woman in me, the corruptible body. Lazarus was called out of the tomb "not simply to go back to his previous life but in order that, having lived through something which cannot be described by any human words, he might re-enter into life with new foundation."

Am I ready to receive such a healing? Am I ready to re-enter the world with an understanding of my renewal? Has such a renewal been effected yet?

1Peter 1: 3-9

> In His great mercy he has given us a new birth into a living hope through the resurrection of Jesus Christ from the dead, and into an inheritance that can never perish, spoil or fade—kept in Heaven for you, who through faith are shielded by God's power until the coming of the salvation that is ready to be revealed in the last time. In this you greatly rejoice, though now for a little while you may have had to suffer griefs in all kinds of trials. These have come so that your faith—of greater worth than gold, which perishes even though refined by fire—may be proved genuine and may result in praise, glory and honour when Jesus Christ is revealed. Though you have not seen him, you love him; and even though you do not see him now, you believe in him and are filled with an inexpressible and glorious joy, for you are receiving the goal of your faith, the salvation of your souls.

I am filled with an inexpressible and glorious joy, mixed as it is at times with tears and sorrow, worry and anxiety. And in the next weeks I will be challenged with all sorts of griefs and trials. I hope that I can open myself to God. I hope that the time away will not be a wasteland of self-indulgent whining and despondency. I want to be light and laughter, hope and love. I want to be me, only better. The essential me. The me that God intended when He formed me in my mother's womb. I don't know how likely that is, in this world, but perhaps I'll see.

November 19, 2007

A Barbaric YAWP!

It might be time for some self-indulgent whining and despondency. The Brits have a lovely word to describe this peevish sort of complaining: whingeing. I need to do a bit of whingeing today. I've tried in vain to be brave and noble, but it will not answer today. Today I want to bellow a barbaric "*Yawp*" to the universe. I don't want to go, I don't want to go, I don't want to go, *I don't want to go!!!!* All weekend I've writhed on my bed in a sleepless agony of dread. I don't want to go to Victoria. I don't want to stay at the Lodge. The very thought of it brings out all the lurking hobgoblins of my past: stumbling social ineptitude, paralyzing shyness, dread of strangers. I know I've changed and grown, that I'm an adult with a certain amount of savoir faire, but in my heart I remain the awkward girl who couldn't look anyone in the face, who panicked in a room of strangers, who hid in the corner twisting her rings, hoping no one would come near, and dreading that no one would.

It's not that I mind being alone. In fact, I like being alone; it has a certain luscious self-indulgence for a mother of young children. All my life, I've treasured, protected and sought alone time. However, I draw the line at being alone with strangers. Especially strangers who have some sort of common bond, where I imagine there might be some kind of cancerous comradeship, where people sit around the communal dinner table with questions hovering on their lips. I know that in prison, it is considered very improper and the height of bad manners to ask why another person is "in." I wonder if it's the same at the Lodge. Do people ask? Do they care? How can I even dare to broach the subject over a plate of cabbage rolls? I class myself with Austen's seemingly cold and elusive Mr. Darcy when I say in his words, "We neither of us perform to strangers."

And it's Christmas. As my niece Crystal said, "Oh, not Christmas ... that's *your* time of year." Yes it is, and thank you for not cloying me up with some sort of "comforting" remark like, "But, they're doing this so that you can spend many more Christmases with your children."

I know. I know I know! Though I am ranting like one at the moment, I am not an idiot. I know this is good for me, that it will make me better, that it will give me my life back. But I can't help but mourn my Now. I want this Christmas. I want my daughter's first school Christmas concert. I want the chocolatey goodness of St. Nicholas Day. I want gingerbread houses, Christmas baking, advent stories, candles and decorating. I want "The Twelve Days of Christmas" bellowed at full voice by my eight-year-old son. I want the light pattering footsteps of my tiny daughter running for the St. Nicholas treats. I want the light train at Stanley Park, the carrousel at Heritage Village, and the lighting of Christmas lights in Campbell River, complete with pipe band and Santa Claus. I don't want the Cancer Clinic up to January 3rd, with only Christmas and Boxing Day off.

I'm not writing this so that people will feel sorry for me—I can do that quite well myself. I just needed to say it. To wallow in my disappointment and grief, my fear and my agony.

I know that my peevishness is due, in part, to lack of sleep: my mind has been a whirling mess of half-formed thoughts and regurgitated worries. My heart and my flesh are failing. "But God is the strength of my heart."

"God *is* the strength of my heart."

"The Lord God is with [me], he is mighty to save. He will take great delight in [me], he will quiet [me] with His love; He will rejoice over [me] with singing." He will quiet my unquiet thoughts ... my roaring, desperate, raving, wild, unquiet thoughts. He will. I need to open my thoughts to Him, and not keep them with frantic, untamed wings huddled against me. Lose them. Let them go. Let them go.

November 19, 2007

Free at Last

Last night I was thrashing around on my bed of unrest, moaning my latest mantra over and over in my head, "I don't want to go ... I don't want to go," when I suddenly caught myself up short. "What am I doing?" I thought. "This way leads to madness." I knew I needed to stop saying it, or even thinking it or I would topple over the edge into the abyss. I need to turn this around; I need to welcome this, to accept it, to anticipate it as I did my surgery. I had been so excited and happy about the surgery, so willing to give my body over to the experience in order that I might rid myself of the cancer, and be healed.

And I've got to do the same now. Open myself. Be welcoming, exhilarated, enlivened. I can no longer moan about the worst that might happen, but rather celebrate the best that might happen. I need to abandon my plans, my dreams, my expectations, my hopes, my children and my Christmas. I can give them up and hope that God will somehow return them to me ... or not—or not in the way I thought, or planned. That might be the whole point: the abandonment of a dream. I've been here before, and I recognize the seemingly barren landscape, devoid of any form or beauty. But there's something just there, over the horizon; and God is going to hold me by the hand until we get there.

Here's what I read this morning: "In my anguish I cried to the Lord, and he answered by setting me free. The Lord is with me; I will not be afraid." As my son would say, "Coincidence? I think not." I am being set free, in ways I can't even begin to understand.

Let It Be

Exploring my thoughts in writing has been so helpful to me over the last few weeks. Sometimes my thoughts get so twisted up by the constant movement around and around my consciousness that I can't get them straight. Just when I begin the mental unravelling, they slip elusively from my grip. But by writing them, I am able to capture them, briefly, and examine them; sometimes in close scrutiny, they lose their power over me—especially those that have seemed most threatening. By removing those, casting them out, disempowering them, the more tender thoughts—the gentle, quiet, hopeful, happy thoughts—have more room to grow. It's a little like gardening. The tender shoots of flowers are there in my garden, but they are invisible until I rout out the virulent weeds that surround and choke them. So, I'm glad I began to write again; I had forgotten the pleasure it gives and the ease it brings.

And I like reading back over what I've written. So often I write in the midst of crisis. I begin in the depths, and squirm around in the muck for awhile until I can begin to make sense of my thoughts, or at least clear them a bit until clarity emerges. Sometimes I never get to the clarity, but it begins a process of looking at that one particular train of thought that is hindering me, or challenging me, or provoking me. At other times, when my thoughts begin the slow spiral again, I can see where they led me last time—and that helps. In the early hours of the morning today, I almost began the "I don't want to go," spiral again. Reading my blog from a few days ago quieted me and gave me back that hard-won perspective I had gained, however transitory.

This week I've struggled with people who want to make me feel better. I think I've been down, and people have seen that and want to cheer me up, jolly me along, give me a biff on the arm.

And so they have "consoled" me with words like, "Your kids are going to be just fine," or "They'll be stronger for this, you know," or "Kids are really resilient—they'll bounce back." Yeah, maybe this is all true—but I've wondered why I'm not allowed to be down, why I'm not supposed to be worried about my children, why I can't be sad. I don't need to feel better. Nothing can really make me feel better. And why should I? This is a sad, hard reality. And more than anything else, I need to be heard. I am voiceless, and unheard when people try to console me. It's like they brush off my words and give me new ones. I say, "I don't think I can deal with any more meals right now, or any more dishes that need returning," and they say, "You can just put them in the freezer, and save them for later." I say, "I don't think I want anyone to stay with me at the lodge," and they say, "You'll really like the company." I say, "I'm worried about being at the lodge," and they say, "Everyone at the lodge is so friendly and kind." I say, "I don't want to leave my children," and they say, "Your kids will be just fine."

I feel like I'm in some weird cone of silence screaming at full lung, but no one hears. It gives me such a sense of powerlessness. We say to children all the time, "Use your words," but what if people won't let you use your words? What then? What recourse is there when words aren't enough? When words can't break through? When you're not allowed to say the deep things of your heart? It's hard enough to admit a weakness or a fear, but it's excruciating when people won't accept them. Somehow I'm left with a sense that what I feel is the wrong thing, that I should be able to magically conjure up those words that other people have put into my mouth. So I end up agreeing, and feeling empty of my self.

And that's a little how I feel about my treatments, too. I dread the first volt of radiation, and the first tablet of chemotherapy medication. I am powerless against the effects of these treatments on my body. It's all about loss of control. Loss of sovereignty. It's about being invaded by courses of toxins that will rove through me destroying and devouring. I know I could choose to say, "No." I don't have to do this ... except that I do. I don't like the odds if I don't: 50% chance of recurrence without the treatment, 7% chance with. I need to do this, but it doesn't stop me from feeling vulnerable, violated. Letting go again—letting go of the sovereignty that was always an illusion anyway.

The people closest to me generally hear me; I'm so fortunate in my friends. Whatever I am at the moment is what they let me be. And I'm so grateful for that—so grateful for them. Grateful for how they hold me and love me and let me be.

One Down; Twenty-four to Go

How do I begin to talk about this day? A couple of days ago I talked about having words, but not being allowed to use them. Today ... I can't seem to capture them. They are fluttering through my consciousness so quickly, I can't catch them. Fleeting, ephemeral, quicksilver words.

Day one at the Cancer Lodge is drawing to a close. At least I wish it were drawing to a close—there are at least three more hours until I can reasonably seek my bed and hunker down for the night. Such a long day—painfully long. And now I hide in the basement of the lodge, both longing for and dreading the night.

What am I doing here? Everywhere I look, I see cancer patients—and it's surreal. It's a whole new level of acceptance of this disease. I suppose it's a good thing to be here, with all these nameless others; it helps me see that I am such a one. A cancer patient. I keep forgetting, or choosing to forget, or ignore, or deny this reality. I say, "I have cancer," with alarming frequency, but I'm always coming up against it in new incarnations. If I just slid into the clinic for my five minute zap, and then rejoined the world, I would be able to live in the fantasy world of wellness; but I live here now at the cancer lodge, where people wear their thinning hair nonchalantly, where a certain gaunt greyness tinges their skin, here in the real world of illness and disease. It's a good place for me to be. Devastatingly difficult, but good. I might be able to achieve a new level of acquiescence here.

Maybe.

I said goodbye to my husband and children with grace and aplomb this morning; I chatted, albeit awkwardly, with Bill the van driver; I squashed myself cheerfully into the back seat of the van with two other riders, one of whom was a rather large and chatty man; I discussed my chemo treatment intelligently with the pharmacist. And then I walked to the lodge. Why is it so difficult for me to enter this place without a tremulous lower lip? I fought back the tears for the whole walk. When I checked in, my voice trembled and my eyes watered. The desk person asked if I wanted lunch. I thought it would taste like ashes in my mouth, so I refused, and just asked for my room. Thankfully my roommate was downstairs in the cafeteria, so I could indulge in a little whingeing blissfully alone. When I finally made it to the lunch room, it was deserted, so I was able to eat my soup alone, while salty tears dropped into my bowl. I felt so alone. More alone than ever in my life, I think.

And all the while a still small voice kept whispering insistently, "You're not alone ... you're *not* alone." Right. I'm *not* alone. "The Lord God is with you. He is mighty to save."

And then my friend Kathy, her face radiating love and comfort, walked in the door. She was in Victoria for the day, and wondered if she could have tea with me and take me to my first radiation appointment. And she asked, rather hesitantly, if I would mind if she and her husband had dinner with me at the lodge. She had been down for treatments in September, and she knew about the first day. She knew.

What a blessing. We laughed, and talked and ate—I ate! And I forgot for an hour where I was and what I was. It was lovely, and I am so grateful. And despite the fact that I still have two hours left until bedtime, I think I'm going to be alright.

God is good. And every day is new evidence that He loves me, and that He knows my heart intimately and that He will provide for every need of my heart before I even think to ask or even know what to ask. How could I know what to ask? My own heart is a mystery to me. But He knew me before the foundations of the world, and He knew about this day. This day when He would care for me as a daddy to a lost and lonely baby girl.

November 28, 2007

Safe from the Storm

I've got to try to relax. It's so difficult for me to be in these forced social situations, where a person might be expected to interact with others. It makes me feel like I need to miraculously transform my personality, and suddenly become a super-social, chatty being. I feel such pressure. I don't really want to initiate conversation, but feel compelled to do so. I begin to see myself as inadequate, and awkward. But today, I decided that I need to let that go, too. As Popeye said, "I y'am what I y'am, and that's all what I y'am." I am at my core quiet, reserved, and introverted; with great effort, and for very short periods, I am able to come out of that and be different, but it's exhausting and I am not able to sustain it for any great time. So, I will do what I do best: smile, listen and watch. That's who I am, and what I do—to try to change for this would be dishonest and futile and fatiguing. I need all of my resources to face this time here—this twenty-five days of soul stripping.

Today was better, but I have to say again that this place is disconcerting. Not only does everyone have cancer, but some have it for the second or third time; it's terrifying. Just when I think I've dealt with the sense of fear and futility, it comes back to haunt me in even greater intensity. Now I live with it, and share a room with it.

Yesterday I met a woman who had "beaten" ovarian cancer ten years ago, but now has a brain tumour. The doctor doesn't like her chances, but is looking forward to being proved wrong. Note: it's the same radiation doctor I have. My roommate had breast cancer seven years ago, and now has lung cancer. She has radiation every day, as well as an hour and a half of chemo. She said something we all think: "If only I knew it was working, I could bear it more easily." Her doctor said that there are no guarantees; but I said that guarantees are what we are all longing for. It's so hard when we can't have the one thing we need to make our lives here more bearable.

At dinner, I saw a girl who couldn't have been more than seventeen. Her bald head was covered in a funky pink scarf, and she wore a really cool, flowing bohemian dress. She looked so beautiful, so young, so fresh. And yet, she is facing something no child should have to face: her own mortality. Maybe for her it's different. Maybe she is so young, she can't even look at the possibility of death. Maybe for her, the cold wind of the grave hasn't blown over her yet. It's different for the older people in the crowd. They know only too well that Death comes knocking—they've felt His cold touch in their bodies for years. But maybe not. Maybe her illness has raised the spectre already.

It's so hard to be here. People are sick, and some are dying. It's hard to know what to do with that. It gets down into my bones and weighs upon me. My heart is so heavy. And yet, this is not a sad place. People laugh, they tell jokes, they gossip over the jigsaw puzzle and cheer over the hockey game. They quilt while resting in the easy chairs, they read bits of the newspaper to each other, they give the nurses a hard time.

To me, it's so surreal. Eternity lurks around the corner, but it's hard to know if anyone sees it. I know that people want to live as though today is not their last day; that death, although a certainty, is not near. But it seems false and unreal. Maybe they are all keeping a brave face for others. I know we all want to keep everyone comfortable and at ease. Maybe the courage and laughter is for others as much as for themselves. I don't know. All I know is that today I needed to be out as much as possible. I needed fresh air, walking, pretty shops, and crowds. You see? I can hide, too. Hide in the silly, frivolous activities that make me forget for a time that I'm here in this place, far from home where everyone is sick and some are dying.

I cling to God, and He holds me close to Him, huddled under His wing, safe from the storms around me, the wild wind of fear and loneliness that howls in my ear and deafens me to His voice. When I run to Him, He lifts His wing, and I scurry under, like a chick afraid of the storm. Nestled close, I hear only the soothing sounds of His heart beat and His quiet words of comfort.

For Lois

I'm sad. So, so sad. I have a heavy weight on my heart, and I don't know what to do about it. And the problem is I don't really understand why I'm so sad. It's a little unexpected, and inexplicable. I am lonely, but I don't think that's it. I miss the warm, loving snuggles of my children, the sweet sound of their laughter, their funny questions and silly jokes—I even miss their irritating wrangling and squabbling. But it's more than missing them, and missing my husband. More than crawling into a cold, comfortless bed at night. I miss *being* someone. I miss my place. Here I am no one—no one's mum, no one's wife, no one's friend. I am no one.

And I don't really have anything to do. I portion my days into little units; thirty minutes for a shower; thirty minutes for lunch (if I remember to bring a book along); twenty minutes to tidy my room. The day is a daunting conglomeration of minutes, and I've never noticed it before. Always before, there have been too few minutes in a day; now there are too many. I'm making my own Christmas cards to help pass the time, but I think I should have brought enough supplies for a hundred cards. I walk, and explore, and think and dream. I carry on imaginary conversations in my mind with friends ... and strangers. I read. I write. Having so much time to think and write might be a dangerous thing—my mind naturally wanders to the melancholy aspects of life. Hence the sadness.

Or maybe it's memory. I keep thinking about Lois. And Shirley. And Melodie. Bright, beautiful, vibrant, loving, dear people who are gone. I can't help but think about them while I'm here, and relive the heartache of their illnesses and deaths. I think I have a lot of unresolved grief about Lois; I don't think I've really mourned for her to the depth I need to. I didn't see her when she was really ill; I didn't see her bald head and wasted frame. Didn't see her when she could no longer hold down a cup of coffee, or lift a book to read. I didn't do anything to care for her, except send Bryan as often as he could go. I had little ones, and Anna was still nursing. We couldn't all go, and I felt at the time that I couldn't leave them behind. For me, her death has always been a little unreal; not even her funeral helped me come to terms with her death. I walked in a haze of complicated and impotent feelings, weird family things and the added stress of caring for my children, who didn't understand what was happening, and who couldn't cope with different sur-roundings, and unknown people. It was a bit of a nightmare. And as a result, I don't think I ever really said goodbye.

But now, I sometimes imagine that I see her here. Here in the faces of older women, bald and frail, enduring an illness they have very little strength or resources to deal with. My heart is pierced. I miss her. She would never have imagined herself to be a person of influence, but she was. My life was so enriched by her presence, her being. She was the most thankful person I have ever met—thankful, grateful, appreciative. And so gener-ous in her praise. I've never really been around a person who told others what she loved about them with such freedom and abandon. I always knew that my parents loved me, but they have never gotten specific. With Lois, it was so different. She had an engaging way of saying exactly what she thought, whatever struck her at the moment. And it was always different. There must have been a hundred and fifty-nine things she loved about me. Sometimes it was sweet and serious, and other times it was just funny. I'll never forget the day we were on a walk at Rebecca Spit. She was behind me, and she suddenly said, "I really like your bum. It's just the right shape: nice and round." And she held her hands just so, to emphasize her point. She said it with no sense at all of having said anything outrageous or uncon-ventional, and her appreciation was so genuine, I could only laugh and hug her to me fiercely. No one has ever loved me so thoroughly ... except her son.

She was an extraordinary woman. So tiny and thin, yet tough, resilient, unflinching throughout a life rife with sorrow and care. Courageous, funny, strong, tender, compassionate, understanding, honest, direct. Inspirational. I loved her, and she is gone.

People say that loved ones are never really gone as long as we remember them. Bollocks. They are gone, and we are diminished.

And so, this is for Lois. I don't really know why I've gone on like this, but strangely I feel better. The knot of grief is loosened a bit. But it is still tangible, and I will have to look at it again. It's okay to look at grief, and to live in it awhile. God is there, and He understands grief better than any.

> If I say, "Surely the darkness will hide me and the light become night around me,' even the darkness will not be dark to you; the night will shine like the day, for darkness is as light to you." Ps 139:11–12

> Though I walk in the midst of trouble, you preserve my life. You stretch out your hand against the anger of my foes, with your right hand you save me. The Lord will fulfill his purpose for me, your love O Lord endures forever—do not abandon the works of your hand. Ps 138:7–8

I am the work of His hand, and He is not finished with me yet—not by a long shot.

December 6, 2007

Belonging

A week since my last post. I intended on writing on the weekend, but exhaustion caught up with me. The kids were wild with excitement on seeing me, and wanted to tell me everything—absolutely everything about their week. On top of that, it was the first weekend of advent, so a certain amount of decorating had to happen, not to mention the baking of gingerbreadmen and sugar cookies. On top of that, it snowed. A lot. Almost two feet. So, of course, that meant endless bundling up, playing outside, unbundling, warming up and starting over again. By Saturday afternoon, all I could do was languish on my couch. I tried not to be crabby, but I don't think I fooled anyone. My poor family.

During the drive home on Friday, I was crammed into the very back seat of the van. A four-hour trip gives a person a lot of time to think. I had already started this line of thought the night before, and just followed it for hundreds of kilometres. Last week I felt so lost, like I wasn't myself, and didn't even know myself. It's been a very long time since I have felt that—I've been pretty secure in who I am and how I interact with the world. I like myself. I'm happy to be me. But not last week. Last week I was spinning like an arrow on a compass, looking for north. I couldn't find it my north. Directionless. Disoriented. Panicked. Lost, with no point of reference. I felt so vulnerable and alone.

Then a strange thing happened. The thing itself wasn't strange, but its effect on me was strange. Someone called me by name. Someone who worked at the clinic called me by name and included me in an activity. The next day, someone else called me by name and talked to me about something unrelated to my illness. Suddenly I felt like a real person again. I felt as though I had come into myself a little bit again. As though I had returned to a place of safety after a long journey away. I think it was then that I was finally able to wrench my eyes away from myself and see—really see—some of the people around me. It struck me that no one wants to be here—it's not a holiday destination for everyone but me. I'm not the only one suffering, and in pain. Shocking that it took me so long to recognize my self-centredness, but I suppose that's what self-absorption means.

I remember resolving to make this ordeal mean something. I don't know if it really means anything or not, but I do know that I can find meaning, or make meaning out of it depending on my response to it all. To live isn't a passive verb, after all—it's an active verb. I can be active—not in an earthshaking, non-Sandy way. But I can offer peace and friendship. I can hold out quietness and grace. I can lift a burden by my smile, and my love. I can do that. I can smile at that quiet woman who seems so alone. I might even be able to sit with her at dinner.

And oddly, when I returned to the lodge today, it felt different to me. People were expecting me. People wondered where I had been and how I was. I had spent a couple of nights in a hotel with my friend, and some people at the lodge had wondered where I was. My roommate from last week had even worried about me and hoped I was okay. Little things, but so crucial to a sense of belonging. So I sat with her at lunch, and we chatted about our weekends, about the snow, about ourselves. It was good. We laughed together. I met my new roommate—I had dreaded a new roommate. But that was okay too.

God provides in mysterious ways. On the drive home on Friday, I had felt my self returning with each kilometre that we drove. I walked into my house and felt restored. I snuggled my children and felt healed. I had communion at church and felt whole. Mysteriously I gained a measure of strength and peace. It will never be easy for me to be here. I will always dislike it and resent it because it pulls me so dreadfully from my true place of belonging. But, God has graciously given me the gift of belonging here in a small measure. I was happy today as I recognized people, and smiled at them and saw that flash of recognition in their eyes. And I am so grateful. And I see now why that sense of belonging is so crucial for inner peace. What about people who never have that, or who had it and lost it? What about them? Children who are abused or abandoned by their parents. Widows. Abandoned husbands. Or wives. Shattered people who have to rebuild their worlds, or who continue to live in fractured places. There is no peace for them, no sense of quietude, no ability to look beyond themselves. No wonder the world is such a sad and sorry place. Such a broken place.

December 7, 2007

The Pitter Patter of Little Feet

I miss my kids so much it's like a physical ache that jars my body when I draw a breath. How can I keep doing this? It's not enough to say that I'll see them on the weekend. It's not enough. I want them every day. Every night. When I call them at night, they scramble to the phone and say, "Mama, Mama," over and over, and I am undone. I can't see them, and I can't touch them; I can only imagine them. And I spent so many years imagining my children that I don't want to do it anymore. I don't want imaginary children; I want real, flesh and blood children who sneak down the hall early in the morning—very quietly so that their father will not hear them and stop them in their tracks—to crawl into my bed and have a snuggle. I want their tug of wars at night to see who gets me first in their bed. I want Christmas books by the fire, Christmas movies in bed, and Alvin and the Chipmunks singing Christmas carols. This is just one thing I cannot be brave about. I've been pretty brave about most things this fall, but I can't do this with a brave smile. Not anymore. I'm plain miserable. I'm glum. And I don't even have any inspiring words to end this blog today. Nothing. I just want my kids.

December 10, 2007

It's All Just a Bad Dream

Last Sunday night I had a very strange dream, but I didn't remember it until yesterday, when I started thinking of heading back to Victoria after an all-too-short weekend.

I dreamt that all of my family and close friends had to have chemotherapy. Horrified at the thought, I said that I would take the treatments for everyone. I remember feeling an urgent need to protect all of the ones I loved, to shield them from the treatments that had already invaded my body. So I said that I would stand in their place; I would take the treatments for them; I would give my body to save them.

In my dream, I crawled into a black van, and drove away. When I arrived at the clinic, a figure opened the door for me. Just as I crossed the threshold, the door swung closed with a clang. Startled, I glanced back, and saw that the door I had just passed through was actually the door to a prison cell. And I couldn't escape. I clung to the bars and screamed for help, but no one heard.

December 10, 2007

They Can't Fire Me, I Quit

Life is just funny sometimes. Last week, I walked into the lodge, and my roommate called me over. I had just met her that morning, and we hadn't really had a chance to talk yet. She was working on the ubiquitous puzzle with a few other women. She asked me if I was going to the nutrition workshop that afternoon.

"That's strange," I said, "I just saw a nutritionist, and she didn't mention a workshop to me."

"Really?" my roommate remarked. "Well, it's a one-hour seminar for all women with breast cancer."

"Oh," I said, somewhat awkwardly, "I don't have breast cancer. I have rectal cancer."

There was a long, uncomfortable silence. People shifted in their chairs, and avoided my eyes.

"Oh," said my roommate, and went back to her puzzle.

I stood there feeling like Rudolph the Red-Nosed Reindeer and Hermie the Christmas Elf must have felt when the King told them they could not live on the Island of Misfit Toys.

"Even among misfits, I'm a misfit."

It made me laugh. A little.

December 13, 2007

A Day in the Waiting Room

Thirteen days out of twenty-five are done: a little over half. It's strange how this has become my life, my place; it's like nothing I have ever imagined, and I have a pretty intense imagination. As I write this, I am sitting in the lounge with twenty-five much older adults listening to the Li'l Jump Band—a "band" consisting of one elderly man on a souped-up, synthesized guitar and his little elderly wife on bass guitar. So far they have played "Tiny Bubbles," "Baby It's Cold Outside," and a jazzed up, almost unrecognizable Nutcracker Suite. Rudolph Nureyev would have a Russian fit if he heard it. I'm not sure if I'll last it out. They are very cute, but I'm a little fragile tonight.

The clinic was an unhappy, traumatic place for me today. No matter how many times I stretch out on that table, I feel queasy and uncomfortable with the thought of the radiation being aimed at my vulnerable body. I feel so exposed. Then, as I was waiting for my doctor's appointment, I met a woman who has to endure twenty-minute radiation sessions, as opposed to my three-minute sessions. Her chest is an almost magenta colour, blistered and itchy; it looks angry and sore. A man was wheeled in on a stretcher. His feeble, wasted arms lifted imploringly to the nurse. I felt sick for him being so exposed in such a moment of weakness in such a public place. Everyone here is so exposed. There is no dignity or privacy. I had to clench my jaw. At night I have to massage my jaws before I go to sleep, I've clenched them so much in the past weeks. I'm trying to break myself of the habit, but something clench-worthy is always coming at me. A man who stays at the lodge had received bad news after his appointment; he sat there, bleak and uncommunicative. I saw the lady who had given me my first tour of the lodge in November. At that time she had just returned as a volunteer after having recovered from her last round of chemo. Today she looked frail and ill—did she have a relapse, I wondered. Did she need more treatments after all? I clenched my jaw again. Is there no end to the pain of this place? The waiting room was dark and dreadful to me today.

And then the doctor. Day after day I am barraged with questions about my most intimate bodily functions. A nurse, then another nurse, then the radiation technicians, then the doctor, then the nutritionist. I know they want to keep track of me, make sure I don't fall through the cracks, help me; but, it does get rather distressing after awhile. And my doctor is so impassive, unemotional and cold. You would think that an impersonal manner might be helpful when discussing such personal matters, but it isn't. It's like trying to seek help from an inanimate object: a chair, or a rock. I feel as though I'm not reaching him, that I'm not able to say what I need to say, that I'm voiceless again, that if I show emotion, it will be really inappropriate and embarrassing. And so I feel trapped by his impassivity.

"How's the skin down there?" he asked. Why is he so loathe to use the real words? He always uses some sort of euphemism, which is much more embarrassing than the real words: "down there," or "pelvic area," or "down below." It makes me feel that I need to be ashamed of my own body—the body I've tried so hard to accept over the last 44 years. And it's very hard to discuss any problems I might be having—like it's unmentionable, and I'm being very inappropriate having these parts, much less discussing them.

"It's a bit itchy," I said.

"I'd better have a look."

"Oh ... really?" I faltered.

"Yeah ... it's easy. Just lean over the bed and drop your pants."

Yeah, it's easy. It's just all so humiliating. I'm not going to have one shred of dignity or privacy left intact. Every day I drop my pants, and crawl onto the radiation table. Every day the technician holds up a sheet to give the illusion of privacy, but it's all smoke and mirrors. Every day they peer intently at my body to find the tattoos, and every day they mistake one of my freckles for a tattoo, and decide to mark my body with a red pen to make the tattoo more visible. And I stay there, impassively, trying not to mind. Trying to blank out what's being done to me without my permission.

So, I dropped my pants and bent over the table. He did what he needed to do and turned away to the sink.

"Looks fine. See you next week." He busied himself at the sink, and didn't turn around. He wouldn't look at me again, and just dismissed me. I was disconcerted, embarrassed. I felt as though I needed to slink away in silence. But, I forced myself to stop, turn to him and say, "Okay, see you next week. Thanks."

If only he had looked at me. Ruefully. Apologetically. Sympathetically. What would it have cost him? Any kind of look would have restored my sense of humanity. But I left feeling empty and sad. Devoid of self-respect. I know he was probably embarrassed himself, probably trying to spare me. But it didn't work.

I needed a long walk in the cold air to restore my equanimity. And it is restored—as much as it can be here.

My roommate taught a mini-class in card-making today. I made three beautiful cards to add to my collection. But more importantly I talked and laughed and created with four other women in pain. That was good. My roommate is a God-send. She knows the names of everyone who stays at the lodge, and she includes me in all her plans. I'm so grateful to her and so thankful that God placed her in my life.

So, good does happen here; sometimes it's just a little hard to find.

December 17, 2007

Counting My Blessings

Written on Friday night:

I've done my share—or perhaps more than my share—of sniveling and complaining in the past 15 weeks or so. But tonight I know that I am a blessed and happy woman. As I write this I am curled up on an elegant winged chair, sipping icy ginger-ale, listening to Musica Intima sing "Ave Maria," and looking at the glittering lights reflected on the still waters of Victoria's Inner Harbour. At my feet is Gwynith and Holly's latest care package spilling out all its treasures; gracing the table beside me is an exquisite flower arrangement sent by three beautiful women whom I know, but haven't seen or spoken to in ages, and wonder how they learned of my whereabouts and the plight in which I find myself. And I'm in this gloriously, wonderfully elegant and restful place because of another gracious and kind friend who loves me.

I find myself feeling more and more like George Bailey, who had to lose almost everything he held dear before he realized that it really was a wonderful life he had. I haven't really lost anything—except perhaps the innocence of health and well-being—but I've certainly been through the grinder. When I look too closely at myself in the mirror, I see all sort of fine lines and stress marks on my face that I didn't notice before: lasting testaments of anxiety, pain, loneliness and fear. I've been sorry, sad, lonely and afraid. I've been embarrassed, confused, humiliated. But looking back, I see the one thing I've been more than anything else; the one thing that covers all the blackness of despair and brings me to humble tears. The one thing that makes me look back with wonder, gratitude and awe—back over everything I've lamented and mourned, so that I can finally see here at the end of myself—the truth that God truly does work everything for good to those who love the Lord, who are called according to

His purpose. The one thing I've been more than anything else is *loved*. And I am humbled, awed and perplexed by it. I know it has so much more to do with the kinds of people my friends are, than with the kind of person I am. And it has so much more to do with the kind of God I love than with anything else. A God who is so much bigger, and more generous than I can ever fathom; a God whose bounty overflows and whose blessings multiply day by day.

When I was baptized, my pastor gave me some verses from Ephesians—I don't want to go find my Bible now, to quote them word perfect—but it's the verses about knowing the love of God: how deep and wide and high and long His love is. How enduring, how personal, how unique and powerful His love is. And I think my whole life has been an exercise in attempting to understand this love. I do not claim to have complete understanding now, but what I do know is that God uses whatever is necessary to bring us to oneness with Him; He uses whatever measures He needs to draw us to Himself and help us understand His character and nature. He has used this present darkness to reveal His love to me. He has used my friends and my church, past students, coworkers, friends from camp from a million years ago—even relative strangers—to reveal His love. And this is all mind-boggling and perplexing. To think that His love for me is so pressing and real.

So now, I will seek my comfy bed, curl under the cozy comforter and attempt to sleep. And if, as is the case too often these days, I have trouble sleeping, I will do what Bing Crosby urged Rosemary Clooney to do in *White Christmas*. "When you're weary, and you can't sleep, just count your blessings instead of sheep, and you'll fall asleep counting your blessings."

December 18, 2007

The Random Moments

I've come to the conclusion that there are no happy days, by which I mean that there are no entire days where happiness reigns supreme—not even entire mornings or afternoons unmarred by conflict or disappointment or unhappiness. This truth has become even more evident to me as children have become a part of my life.

I've always had hugely unrealistic expectations of life. My anticipation of events has always exceeded reality and I've had to learn how to deal with the disappointments of unmet expectations. This past weekend was no exception. I had eagerly anticipated a reunion with my family—and to spend it in beautiful Victoria at Christmas time seemed sheer bliss. But after the initial euphoria and excitement had waned, things quickly went pear-shaped (a British term which means out-of-sorts, or hay-wired.)

In my fondest dreams, I imagined my family and me frolicking merrily through Victoria's Christmas delights: the parade of trees at the Empress, the splendour of Craigdarroch Castle, the Festival of Lights at Butchart Gardens. I did not imagine truculent, exhausted children squelching my every plan for their amusement.

"I don't want to go look at Christmas trees."

"Do we have to leave the hotel?"

"I want to go swimming."

"I don't want to go swimming, I want to play racketball."

Argh!!!

Part of the problem is that we haven't really been a family for over three weeks—we have been fragmented, separated, broken. For each reunion, we have needed to heal the breach, and it has gotten harder and harder to do as the children have become more distressed, more sleepless and more hurt by the separation. And—now used to endless hours of solitude and silence—I've had to drag myself reluctantly back to the world of noise and responsibilities. It's wrenching and emotional and difficult. In our stressed-out, traumatized, exhausted states, the weekend together was unexpected. I did not expect the difficulties, and found it all a bit demoralizing and depressing. And I'm sure my children felt the presence of the black cloud of disappointed dreams.

Having said all that, it was a good weekend. There were moments that sparkled with delight and laughter.

My daughter woke from a nightmare on Thursday night and turned in bed to find me beside her. "Mummy," she murmured delightedly, "It's you. You're here."

My son reluctantly agreed to a trip to Butchart Gardens to see the lights. Once there, he became new; he ran around enthusiastically and said, "I guess it would be fun to find the 12 days of Christmas ... but we have to find them all ... in order!"

And my daughter, "Mummy, look at the twinkliness of it all!"

Glittering, twinkling moments of delight. Moments where happiness reigned supreme.

My daughter looking at me with stars in her eyes after sitting on Santa's knee. "Mummy, he asked if I was trying to be good. And I said that I am trying. Mummy, I love Santa. I just know he loves Jesus."

Having a heated argument with my son over something very silly, and then both collapsing in helpless laughter over a very bad pun. And walking hand in hand to look at the real reindeer at

Santa's workshop.

"Froot Loops for breakfast? Really? Mum, you're the best!"

"Mummy, I've never been to a for-real castle before. Will there be a princess inside?"

"As soon as you go in, there will be, Darling."

"Oh, Mummy, you're so silly."

Yes, I am silly. I'm silly for almost missing those moments: those unanticipated, spontaneously delightful moments that spring on a person unannounced and unexpected. Silly for fretting over those other moments that will not bend to my rigid expectations and plans and that threaten to extinguish my joy and rob me of the delight found in the random moments of life.

December 18, 2007

The Truth of the Matter

I feel like a little kid sitting in the back seat of the car during a long journey. "Are we there yet? Are we there yet?" I keep thinking that at any moment I'm going to get there—anywhere. That the endless trip will be over and I will be able to rest. But, it ain't over. There's always a more grueling stretch lurking around the corner.

I finally had the courage to ask my oncologist about my future. I had been wanting to ask for awhile, but had never been able to screw up my courage to the sticking point. I wanted to know, "What next?" But, I'm kind of sorry I asked. Knowledge is not necessarily power; sometimes it's just knowledge.

She told me about the "souped-up" version of chemo I'm going to receive in January. I had thought I was going to just carry on with the pills I've been taking, but at a stronger dosage. But instead, I will need to have a PICC line, and a portable pump that I will have to have with me for 48 hours at a time. The PICC line will stay in for the duration of the chemo (15 weeks). I must have gone a little green around the gills.

"You remember me talking about this," she said.

No. I didn't remember. I'm sure I would have remembered the PICC line.

She went on, "In the case of high-risk cancers like yours, we want to be as aggressive as possible."

I did a double-take.

"Did you say, 'high-risk'?"

"Yes, yours is a high-risk cancer because it likes to grow back in the same place."

The room tilted and a roaring filled my ears. I had never heard anyone use the term "high-risk" before, and I didn't know what to do with it. With teary eyes, I looked at the doctor and said, "Okay, we need to talk about this. I need to know what my future looks like." So, for the next hour, she drew pictures and charts and scribbles, and told me what I need to know. It was heart-wrenching and exhausting. Yesterday I wrote about my expectations and plans, and how life rarely meets my expectations. I had planned on 15 weeks of chemo in pill form—easy, non-invasive, unthreatening. But instead, I'm to receive a PICC line on my upper arm and a harsher cocktail of drugs. I feel too tired to deal with this; my body is beginning to rebel against the assaults made against it. I'm exhausted, nauseous and depressed. The radiation tech had to press tissues into my hand today before she left the room; I couldn't make my lips stop trembling, or my eyes stop watering.

I feel a little like I am flying to pieces. And I won't be able to coalesce again. I'll just remain little pieces of me jumping around, unable to cope with life.

It's just that it's unexpected. A PICC line is not a horrible thing. The chemo is not that hard to live with. The extra treatment gives an additional 10% chance of success. I just don't really want to talk about numbers or success rates or statistics after all. I just want to be better, and to go home and to be me again. I don't want to have a "high-risk" cancer and to have years ahead of me in which I face test after test, scan after scan wondering if this is the time they'll find a spot on my lung or my liver. I don't want to come here again.

Yesterday I wanted to know the truth, I needed to hear it. Today I want to run from it and be free, but there is no freedom for me. Not yet.

2008

January 2, 2008

The Weak and the Strong

I'm so, so tired. I can't ever remember being so tired in all my life—not even when I was pregnant, and that's saying something. I came home for a five-day break at Christmas, and spent most of my time in bed, or on the couch. I was so fragile and weepy that I didn't recognize myself. Hardly a moment passed when I wasn't tearing up over something or other. *But ...* it was so lovely to be home, and hold my children close. We snuggled in bed at every opportunity. And when they could be pried away, they would run down the hall every few minutes to check that I was still there. It was very sweet, but heart-wrenching at the same time.

A couple of conversations with my son, aged eight:

Me: (holding him close) "Oh, there's nothing better than an arm full of Nathan."

Him: (with a strangle-hold on me) "Yes, there is—an armful of Mummy."

Last Christmas night:

Me: "Did you have a good Christmas, Darling? Did you like your presents."

Him: (long pause, then with a slightly wobbly voice) "I did, Mummy. ... But the best present of all was having you home. I love you."

My heart. How can I bear it? Sometimes, when they are not aware, I catch them looking at me with such anxiety. Am I going to leave again? Will I return? Will I spend the rest of my life in bed, or in the tub, or in the bathroom? Will I ever play with them again, or cook a meal, or be normal in any way? And I have nothing to say. Today, I feel as though I'll never feel well again. I'm so tired.

I finished my treatments on Monday, Dec 31. I wanted to be glad, and celebrate, but all I could do is fall into an exhausted sleep, swallowing hard against the nausea. They said the side effects would last for up to two more weeks. They'll start up the chemo on Feb 4.

On Sunday, I felt so hopeful; so sure that I was going to be able to finish this well. But today, I'm just too tired to do anything well, except perhaps complain.

God holds me in the palm of His hand. I know that. I do. He is refining me by removing the dross. But I'm afraid that if He whittles much more away, there won't be much left.

Maybe that's the point. Paul said, "When I am weak, then He is strong." I'm so weak. I'm so weak. I'm so weak.

January 2, 2008

My Hiding Place

I'm a little ashamed of myself today. I gave way to despair last night; I really have to stop watching late-night movies about mothers who die of cancer. Last night Stepmom was on TV: I tried to avert my eyes, change the channel, stop myself—but I couldn't. It was like driving past an accident site: you know you'll be sorry; you know you will carry the image of twisted metal and crushed windows for the rest of the day; you know the pictures will invade your dreams, but you just can't look away. That's how it was last night. I kept thinking, "This is a mistake. Turn it off. Don't watch." But I didn't listen to my better judgement. I did turn it off before the mother died, but I'd seen enough. Stupid, stupid, stupid. However. Today the sun is shining. My tummy feels more settled. I am determined to rise from my bed, and maybe even get some fresh air. But more to the point, I spent a lot of time talking to God last night. Well, "talking" might be misleading. I did a lot of crying out incoherently, sobbing convulsively—you know. But God doesn't mind that. Sometimes I think that the more incoherent our prayers, the better; that's when the Holy Spirit really takes us to the heart of God. When I don't have any words, there's nothing to get in the way. There's nothing but my heart laid bare before God. In church on Sunday, a few verses really struck me. The pastor had been talking about suffering—you know I was listening intently—and he referred to the suffering of Paul. "We were under great pressure, far beyond our ability to endure, so that we despaired even of life. Indeed, in our hearts we felt the sentence of death. But this happened that we might not rely on ourselves but on God who raises the dead. He has delivered us from such deadly peril, and he will deliver us. On him we have set our hope that he will continue to deliver us ..." I certainly do not class myself with Paul, except in the sense that we are both flawed people loved by God. My "deadly peril" is different from his, and yet I feel that I can gain much insight and strength from his experience. My "deadly peril" is the temptation to forget God; to wallow in my despair and never allow myself to be lifted out; to forget that God is a sovereign God who loves me and has a design for my life; to bear my grief alone and not seek the comfort of the One who made me and knows me better than I know myself; to forget that what He wants most is my heart, and that I need to trust Him with my heart, my life, my children and my future. So today, or for this moment, it is well with my soul. He is my hiding place.

January 3, 2008

For Bryan

Here's part of a telephone conversation between Bryan and me on Dec. 20th. Bryan was in Campbell River, I was still in Victoria:

Sandy: "Hi, Honey, how are you?"

Bryan: "I'm okay. ... I took the kids out for dinner tonight."

Sandy: "Great! Where did you go?"

Bryan: "Wendy's. ... I feel like such a failure."

Sandy: *"What? Why?"*

Bryan: "I couldn't even cook dinner for my kids two nights in a row."

This from the man who has single-handedly cared for our children with patience, kindness, compassion and tenderness for almost six weeks. The man who got them up in the morning, cooked their breakfast, made their lunches, brushed their teeth, found their clothing, organized their library books and homework and still managed to get out of the house on time. Well, almost on time. I suspect there were one or two days when the three of them did what Bryan calls "The flip, flop and fly." Flip out of bed, flop on some clothes and fly out the door.

This is the man who continued to work full-time, and fulfill his responsibilities at work while carting kids to dance lessons, play dates, clubs and piano lessons. The man who bought groceries, did laundry, tidied the house before I came home on the weekend, and catered to my every whim when I returned, exhausted on Friday nights. And all this without a word of complaint. Not a word. Not a moment of self-pity. Not a whinge.

Where do you find such a man?

When Bryan was a small boy, he loved to play make-believe. He was always the hero who saved the damsel in distress. Very seldom do a person's dreams of make-believe come true, but Bryan's did. He *is* the hero. And I am the damsel in distress.

Oddly, when I was a little girl, I dreamed of being rescued by the hero. I pictured him riding up and vanquishing the evil forces holding me captive, and then sweeping me away in his protective arms. I guess my make-believe came true, too. Bryan can't really vanquish the bad guy in this scenario, but he has rescued me and protected me, and held me safe. He has rescued my children, loved them and nurtured them even better than I could have done in similar circumstances.

I have often said in the last few weeks that it's a good thing it's me that's sick. I could never do what Bryan has done with such grace, such patience and such goodness. He radiates strength.

He would probably disagree with me. I know he has felt several times as though he was barely hanging on, that everything was going to fly apart at any second. And it's true that little things have gone awry. It is true that our daughter showed up a school a couple of times without socks, in the middle of a raging southeaster. It is true that when they came down to meet me in Victoria for the weekend, Nathan had seven shirts, four pairs of pants, no pj's, no socks, and no winter coat; and our daughter had two shirts, one pair of pants, one dress and one skirt—none of which matched—and no tights, three pairs of shoes and two nightgowns. Oh, and no hair brush—but that was probably a good thing, since her hair clearly hadn't been brushed all week, and the tangles would have been beyond a mere brush's ability to deal with. But the truth is that things go awry with me in charge, too—only I get everyone all twisted up about it, while Bryan just shrugs. And everything is just fine.

And all this time, he has made fresh bread for me, to tempt my appetite; he has brought me hot water bottles to warm me up; he has rubbed my tender feet, gotten the knots out of my back, and stroked my forehead when I was sad.

A couple of weeks ago, a friend gave me a book called *Porn for Women*. Every page has a beautiful man doing something that women find sexy—like doing the laundry, or cooking a meal, or filling a bubble bath for them. One has a man holding out a piece of cake, saying "Have another piece of cake ... I hate to see you looking so thin." Another has a man emptying the clothes dryer saying, "As soon as I'm done the laundry, I'll go get groceries ... and I'll take the kids with me so you can have a break."

I don't need *Porn for Women*. I live it, Baby.

Our son once chose these words to express what he thought of when he thought of his daddy:

> *Love is patient, love is kind. It does not envy, it does not boast, it is not proud. It is not rude, it is not self-seeking, it is not easily angered, it keeps no record of wrongs. Love does not delight in evil but rejoices with the truth. It always protects, always trusts, always hopes, always perseveres. Love never fails.* 1 Corinthians 13:4-8

That's my Bryan.

January 12, 2008

I Saw Eternity before Me, a Ring of Endless Light

Before I begin, I just need to preface this by saying that I'm feeling really good, as though I'm finally returning to myself. My taste buds are restored, I'm enjoying my meals, and I'm sleeping better.

However.

I have been thinking a lot about suffering lately: the nature of pain and suffering, even the side effects of pain and suffering (since side effects seem to be occupying my every waking moment these days.) Elie Wiesel said, "Suffering contains the secret of creation and its dimension of eternity. ... suffering betters some people and transfigures others. At the end of suffering, of mystery, God awaits us." If anyone ever knew about suffering, Elie Wiesel did. In his book, *Night*, Wiesel describes himself as an adolescent, huddling silently in the darkness while the Nazi guards at Auschwitz tortured his father to death. I don't know if Wiesel was transfigured by his suffering or not, or if he was able to find God at the end of it all. But I do know that the idea of transfiguration, or transformation by suffering is a theme I've returned to again and again over the last few months.

I think so often in our lives we flee from pain and suffering; we eschew it, as my friend Shannon would say. And in the evangelical Christian church, we do worse: we "cast it out," we "rebuke it in the name of Jesus." We think that if God loves us, we won't be sick, or sad, or pain-ridden. Or, worse yet, we cast blame and issue condemnation: "If your faith were stronger, you wouldn't be sick." "If you really believed, God would heal you."

Bollocks.

There is this pervasive fallacy floating around that says that God wants us to be well and happy and prosperous. Rot. He has never said that He wants us to be happy. What He wants is for us to be His. Without reservation. And He orchestrates our lives in such a way as to give us opportunities to become His in an ever deeper, ever more mysterious way.

Let me be perfectly clear. I do not want to suffer; pain is not something I choose, whether it be physical or emotional. In the past, I have always avoided pain, run from it, refused to face it. But the problem with running away is that I have to take myself along, and all my failures and shortcomings tag along for the ride. There were times I could choose to run and hide, but that doesn't seem to be an option now, nor would I want it to be. I've come to see the whole problem of pain in a different light.

Rather than run from the pain, I need to turn to it. Embrace it. Surrender to it, and see where it leads me. At this point, it's not really physical pain: any discomfort I have experienced has been unpleasant, but bearable. But, exhaustion is wearing. The seemingly endless days of treatment stretch before me, and I often wonder how I will endure to the end. I whinge and moan. I worry about being a burden to my friends. I fret over the fragility of my body, and the vulnerability of my spirit. I contemplate the future, and the 75% chance of complete cure. I look into the eyes of my doctors, and implore them to give me a guarantee that they cannot in good conscience give. I don't really have a sense of the future, beyond this appointment, or that set of treatments, and that is something I find very difficult. I read somewhere that "Possessing a sense of the future is vital to feeling whole." Maybe that explains a bit of my sense of fractured-ness.

Emotional suffering is no less real than physical, and there are fewer solutions. But value can be found in suffering: some truths can only be gained through sorrow; sometimes it is only through suffering that we can come to an understanding of self, and an understanding of life, death, and eternity.

In the weird dichotomy that is Christianity, there is a link between suffering and wholeness; between loss and gain: "For
anyone who wants to save his life will lose it; but anyone who
loses his life for my sake, and the sake of the gospel, will save it"
(Mark 8:35). Thomas Merton said, "In order to become myself
I must cease to be what I always thought I wanted to be, and
in order to find myself I must go out of myself, and in order to
live I have to die."

So, in the endless waiting that is my life right now, I find myself
turning over in my mind questions about the nature of life, of
love, of pain, of eternity. Bernard of Clairvaux said, "Life is
only for love. Time is only that we might find God." I want to
live a life of love, even when it might seem ridiculous to others,
or misunderstood. And I pray for enough time—for me, for my
children, for my family and friends. Time to find God.

January 12, 2008

Waiting

I'm reading a book right now that a friend sent me. It's called *Facing Death. Discovering Life.* As you can imagine, it's a hard read.

I don't feel like I'm going to die. Not today, anyway. But I will, one day. And the greatest gift inherent in facing a serious illness, is that it gives you pause to think. And time to think. So much of my experience over the last four months has been a seemingly endless series of waits. Waiting for test results, waiting for surgery, waiting for appointments and procedures, waiting for treatments. I used to hate waiting; I'd fidget impatiently in the waiting rooms, flipping irately through limp magazines. But a couple of years ago, I came to see waiting in a different light. I saw it as a respite, a brief moment in which to rest, to think, to be still in body and mind.

Now so much of my life is consumed with waiting; at the moment I am waiting for my body to recover and regain strength so that I can begin my next round of treatments. And it's a little disconcerting to be waiting in relative stillness while the world all around bustles with activity. I'm always sort of fighting the urge to be up and doing. "To live" is an active verb, and it is strange to be in-active. Every afternoon, I take my daughter to Kindergarten, and then find a place where I can go to rest, a place other than my own home; if I returned home, I know I would bustle, and work, and exhaust myself with the minutiae of housekeeping that is both my bane and my delight. And so I sit in Starbucks, drink my latte, and watch the world go by.

Waiting can be exhausting, especially if I spend it in too much speculation of the future, if I allow the clouds of dread to gather into a tempest.

DAMNED NEAR KILLED HIM

Waiting can be lonely: extended periods of solitude locked in an experience that is not easily shared by those outside. I have loads of loving support, but no one—not even my husband—is really inside. He is inside his own experience, and faces his own isolation and loneliness, as do my friends who often have to wait helplessly, with hands at their side through it all.

And yet, these times of waiting that I used to dread, used to consider a terrible waste of time, have become in many ways my salvation. A time of listening to and acknowledging my inner-most fears; of facing my self; of seeking God and hearing His still, small voice; of affirming life, and anchoring my soul. "Deep calls to deep" in the waiting room.

Lines Written in a Starbucks

Someone asked me the other day if I had learned anything during my time in Victoria, if I had gained any insights into life. And then he waited. In silence. One of the things I love best about this man is his gift for silence. If I had asked that question of someone, and then faced several moments of dead air, I would have been hard-pressed not to answer my own query—not to fill the void with my own voice. But not Tony. He just waited.

After a moment or two, I said, "Yes, I think I have learned something."

"What? What is it?" he pressed.

I've learned that life is both richer and sadder than it was before.

Richer because I've been challenged to enter into the heart and depth of things that I only danced around before. I've gained a sense of wholeness, a measure of peace in the midst of this particular happening in my life. I've been loved by others as deeply and as completely as it is possible for human beings to love. I've relinquished my yen for control and my desire to captain my own ship. I've let myself fall into the arms of others, and trusted myself to them in ways I never knew I could. And that vulnerability has been incredibly powerful and beautiful. To allow another to love me and care for me is very frightening, especially for someone as intensely private and obsessively independent as I am. But it is so freeing. So healing. I guess surrendering to God's will in life also means surrendering to His will in death. Death of self.

Odd, really, that it is in moments of intense physical and emotional suffering that I have found healing; been transformed through pain and dependence: utter dependence on others, and utter dependence on God. Another paradox. It reminds me of John Donne's poem, *Batter My Heart, Three Person'd God*.

> Batter my heart, three person'd God; for you
> As yet but knocke, breathe, shine and seek to mende;
> That I may rise, and stand, o'erthrow mee, and bend
> Your force to breake, blow, burn and make mee new.
> I, like a usurpt towne, to another due,
> Labour to admit you, but Oh, to no end,
> Reason your viceroy in mee, mee should defend
> But is captiv'd, and proves weak or untrue.
> Yet dearely I love you, and would be loved faine,
> But am betroth'd unto your enemie:
> Divorce mee, untie, or breake that knot againe;
> Take mee to you, imprison mee, for I
> Except you enthrall mee, never shall be free,
> Not ever chaste, except you ravish mee.

Unless I am enthralled by God, imprisoned by Him, utterly dependent on Him, I never shall be free.

So, in the midst of all this, life *is* richer because I can see into its centre more clearly than I could before. I know better what it is that makes life sweet and delightful and worth the pain.

But, life is also sadder. I told Tony that I felt my innocence was gone. The illusion of health and youth has been stripped away. It always has been an illusion, but I was fooled; I didn't see the man behind the curtain until I got sick. And so now, when I do think of the future, it is always tinged with melancholy. Family celebrations, birthdays, plans for holidays and trips always have festoons of shadows drifting around the edges. A deep awareness of the fleeting nature of life is with me like it never has been before. It is not oppressive, but it is always there, and that saddens me. More questions, and fewer answers. But I can live with that.

January 23, 2008

More of the Same

So, I'm sitting here in Starbucks (again), trying to figure out why I feel so upset. I knew the chemo was coming: it's not a surprise. And yet, I feel sort of taken aback, caught off guard. Gobsmacked. I think what happened is that I got used to feeling well, and maybe had begun to think that the worst was behind me. And maybe it is. But maybe it isn't. Or maybe it's another kind of worst coming.

I went to see the chemo nurse yesterday, to talk about my next round of treatments. It was a little weird. I had taken her a lovely bunch of tulips—the sun was shining, and the tulips were so pretty in the store, that I *had* to buy them—and as the nurse walked up to me, she held out her hand to shake mine in greeting. Instead of shaking her hand, I held out the bunch of tulips for her to take. She looked a little nonplussed, and I immediately felt as though I had made a terrible faux pas, so as we entered the room, and she put the flowers on her desk, I hastened to say, "I didn't mean *not* to shake your hand." We shook hands, and then she did something very odd. She hurried over to the sink, and washed her hands with anti-bacterial soap. I was startled. I don't *think* I'm contagious. I don't *think* rectal cancer is catching. Hmmm.

I guess she has to be pretty careful about germs.

And then we began talking about my PICC line, or *port*. She explained that there are two ways of doing one: in the upper arm, or in the chest. "For you, we'll probably do the upper arm. We don't *really* expect you to have to come back. Some people we know will have to come back and do this again sometime. But we don't really expect that you'll have to come back."

Silence. Stunned, on my part. Don't really expect ... I wanted to yell, "Damned right, I'm not going to come back and do this again! I am *not* going to *have* cancer again, do you hear me??!! Well? Do you?!!" Of course, I said nothing of the sort. I just gripped my trembling lip between my teeth, and said nothing. She handed me a box of tissues, and sort of groaned, "I should *not* have said that ... Why did I say that?"

Argh. Just when I was feeling settled ... and happy ... and hope-hope-hopeful (as I said to Tony, after three attempts at the word), my underpinnings are knocked out from under me again.

And then we talked about the drugs. Not the chemo drugs, but the drugs I need to take to cope with the chemo drugs. I showed her the prescription my oncologist had written in November, before the funding came through for the more aggressive treatment. Silence. Again.

"Yeah ... These aren't really going to do the trick. You're going to need something a lot stronger, at least for the first few days after each treatment. Oh, and you'll be taking dexamethasone, too."

"Huh?"

"It's a steroid. It will pep you up and make you feel like doing things. It's great. It's gotten a bad rap, but some people like it so much, they continue to take it throughout the treatments."

I went home and looked it up on the internet. Oh, it's great, alright: 6 to 10 times the strength of prednisone. Nice. My roommate in Victoria took it during her chemo, and gained twenty pounds. It's great alright. It's not that I mind gaining weight—but to gain it because a steroid is raging through my body, "pepping" me up and make me gorge myself, doesn't sound very enticing.

Okay. I lied. I *do* mind gaining weight. This whole cancer thing has wreaked havoc on my body and my psyche. Before all this happened, I was feeling pretty happy about myself—a peace with myself that was only gained through years of learning how to love and accept myself regardless of the size number on my pants, or the figure on my scale. In fact, in all my adult life, I have never owned a scale, and (apart from two pregnancies), have refused to weigh myself. I spent too many years obsessed by numbers, and needed to break free from it all. And in the last few years, I think I have gained some real liberty. Some love.

But now, I'm all messed up. It's very hard to keep myself sorted out when so many well-meaning people approach me and say, "Wow! You look great!" or "Gosh, you look fantastic!" or "I think you've come up with a weight loss plan that works" or even, "You've always wanted to lose weight, and now you look really good." All genuine comments made to me in the last four months. And all made after what I call an "elevator" look that starts at the top, moves slowly down the body, and then back up again. I've lost over twenty pounds, and am sporting what I call my "Cancer Chic" look.

I've been assured by a friend that I am not "skinny"—nor do I think I am. But it's very confusing for me to be complimented on a weight loss that came only as a result of a grueling surgery, six weeks of radiation and chemo, and the accompanying side effects: severe intestinal cramping, nausea, loss of appetite and diarrhea. And I do know that some people compliment me because my colour is good, and I look reasonably healthy and well—but others ... *oy!*

I don't really know why this of all things is bothering me right now; why it's become such an issue to me. But it has. Maybe it's just the thought of another assault on my beleaguered body. Maybe it's that whole notion of loss of control, and voiceless-ness over what is done in and to my body. Can I choose NOT to take some of these drugs? What will happen? I just feel that my body is being bounced all over the map, and I'll never attain equilibrium again. I think that's really what this is about. I'm just beginning to feel well, and whole, and happy. And it's all an illusion that's about to be shattered.

It makes me feel sad. And hope-hope-hopeless.

January 26, 2008

My Doom Is Come upon Me

I went to the Cancer ward at the hospital today. I wanted to get a few more details about my PICC line and my treatments—particularly the hideous drugs used to combat the hideous chemo drugs. It's so crazy. I don't really want to take a steroid, and I had hoped I would be able to talk to the nurse, and negotiate a bit. I would rather *not* take the steroid at first, but take the prescription home and take it if I need it. I would rather see if there is something natural I could do—maybe something that my homeopath could recommend. But when I broached the idea, the nurse just said, "Oh, you're going to take the dexamethasone."

"Do I have to?" I asked.

"Yeah ... You do. You are going to take some before the treatment, then we are going to send some home, and you are going to take more. Then you are going to journal what is happening in your body. You might end up in the Emergency Ward that night, vomiting. And then we'll give you even more."

"Oh," I said, rather lamely. "Okay, then."

"You know, we don't *want* to give you more drugs than you need, but we don't want you vomiting."

I guess I don't really want that either. As Bryan would say, "I'm unanimous" about that.

So I left, feeling pretty stupid, and whiney, and stupid.

Later in the day, I took Anna out for lunch. At the restaurant, I saw a woman who was at the lodge in Victoria. She was just finishing her radiation as I was starting. We exchanged compliments, and then asked each other what was next. When I told her that I was about to start chemo, her face crumpled.

"Oh, I don't envy you *that* ... I *hated* chemo," and she shivered.

All-righty, then.

January 26, 2008

One More Thing

I just need to say one more thing. When I talked about being annoyed with people giving me compliments, and telling me I looked good, I wasn't talking about my friends, who are genuinely glad that I look healthy and well, despite the last few horrific months. I'm glad, and grateful when people tell me this: I feel loved, and supported by this. I feel that maybe I don't look as haggard, and drawn, and fragile as I feel. That maybe, I can walk around town, and that I don't have a sign on my forehead that reads, "I have cancer, pity me." When I was complaining so bitterly the other day, I was referring to people who compliment me *because* of the weight loss. I find *that* really hard to bear, and I don't know what to say in response. Because, in truth, the weight loss scares me a little bit, or it did—when I wondered if I would ever *stop* losing weight, or if I would continue going in every week having lost a pound or two. I had a wretched taste in my mouth, I couldn't eat, I was lonely and afraid. *That's* when those comments ate away at me. Now, I don't care so much. I feel good, I'm eating, and I've put on a couple of pounds. I just worry that it will start up again with the chemo. In fact, I'm sort of beside myself. I toss in my bed at night wondering just how awful I'm going to feel. I can hardly think of anything else, and I wonder how I can stand waiting until it begins. It's the waiting that is so debilitating. And I don't want to be complimented over something that has caused me so much anxiety, and confusion.

That's all.

January 27, 2008

Someone Else's Story

I've come to the conclusion that we can never really enter someone else's pain; and they can never enter ours. I'm not talking about me today; I'm not whining because I think that people don't understand my pain, or aren't able to help me through my hard times: this *isn't* about my pain, for a change. No, I'm thinking about other people I know, who are facing horrific moments in their lives, and my inability to enter into their experience. My friends have been unbelievably great at coming alongside me, and meeting me in my darkness—I don't know how they do it. I feel like with other people, I might think I get it, and might even get a flash of understanding, or true empathy, but not enough. We never really see the whole picture of a person's life, do we? We are strangers, blindly bumping into each other in the dark. We wander around the periphery of each other's lives, wringing our hands and praying that somehow we can break through the pain for a brief minute, and touch another's heart, however lightly. My friends have touched my life in profound and intimate ways, but I don't think I could really explain *how* they've done this, or *what* they've done. I feel helpless and sometimes hopeless as I wait for the clouds to lift enough to permit me access into another's life.

And it's so much more difficult to witness the pain of someone we love, than to suffer our own pain. Our own pain is something we sort of understand; we know its parameters, so to speak; in some ways we have defined it, and have found some sort of peace within it. So, even though pain is present, suffering is held at bay. But with another person, we just don't know: it's all such a mystery. We don't know the extent of their suffering; we don't know if they have found any peace within it, or if they have heard the voice of God, or even if they *want* to hear it.

I have a few friends (some just acquaintances), facing some really hard things. From the outside, I just can't see how they will be able to work through it, how they will be able to cope. A darling friend whose beloved mother is desperately ill. A new mom, whose twin babies have come into this cold world far too early. Another friend recently diagnosed with cancer. A wife, whose talented, intelligent husband can't find a job. Another marriage that has fallen apart.

This is a cold, unhappy world, where pain heaps upon pain. I don't know why I keep finding myself surprised by this, but I do. I keep thinking, naively, that the world is a good and happy place: I've always been a glass-is-half-full kind of girl. But the longer I live, the more I understand that this world is indeed "a vale of tears." I don't really ask "Why?" when something happens to me. I might pout, or get angry, or whine, but I don't often question. *But*, when it happens to someone else, the questions fly. "Why would God allow someone to become pregnant, only to lose the baby weeks later?" I don't get it. I don't get why a seventeen-year-old would have to die a lingering death, or why children would have to lose both a mother *and* a father to cancer.

I don't get it.

And I never will.

Not in this lifetime, anyway.

In my own life I've found a certain measure of resignation and surrender: an acknowledgement of the sovereignty of God. But it's hard to have that for someone else. And so, I wander around the periphery, lost for words, desperate to help, yet helpless.

I need to accept that God is at work in more lives than just mine, and that His work is supremely mysterious. People looking at me might say, "Why does she have to have cancer? A mum, with two small children? What's going on?" From the outside it makes no sense (from the inside, the sense is sometimes hard to decipher as well). But I do believe that God can take something tragic and unhappy, something twisted and wrong, and turn it to something good. I can believe that in my life, because I can see how it is so. And I can hope and pray that God is at work in the lives of others, too.

As Aslan says in *The Horse and His Boy*, "Child ... I am telling you your story, not hers. No one is told any story but their own."

February 5, 2008

The Wrong Way Around

On December 31, 2007, the day I finished my radiation treatments in Victoria, Laurie and I stopped in Duncan to have lunch on the way home. Why Duncan? We were too tired, and we couldn't wait until Nanaimo. The whole trip had already been too daunting, and I was so tired, worn, fragile and ill to face more than 45 minutes in the car at a time. But we didn't stop at a fast food place on the strip of highway through town— my whole body rebelled against it; so, we ferreted out a fabulous little organic foods restaurant. Funky, cool decor and a killer menu. I couldn't do much more than sip my ginger ale, and nibble my sandwich, but it is a place I will have to visit again. When we left, we noticed a shoe store next door. A very un Duncan-ish shoe store.

A wild, outrageous, sexy little store with wilder, more outrageous shoes.

And boots.

And it advertised a clearance sale.

How could we resist? Wracked with nausea, trembling with intestinal cramps, reeling with fatigue, I followed Laurie into the store. She immediately found a luscious pair of red half-boots that had her salivary glands working overtime. And asked for her size. And was disappointed, when none of the sizes available was hers.

I glanced around a little more slowly. Didn't know if I even had it in me to slip off my shoes, and enter the game.

"Wait," I said to the clerk (who wore more red spandex than I'd seen since 1985), "What sizes do you have in those boots?"

DAMNED NEAR KILLED HIM

Mine.

I think I may have been delirious with fatigue, or nausea, or something. I bought the boots. Ridiculously high heel, and flashy red uppers and buckles and all. What was I thinking?

When I got home and took them out of the bag, I blenched a little—they are so very red. So very buckled.

But I wore them. With skirts. In the snow. On every possible occasion.

One day I wore them to take Anna to Kindergarten. The teacher's assistant squealed, "Oh! I *love* your boots."

As I thanked her, rather deprecatingly, she continued, "Those are the boots of a very confident woman."

Ouch.

"Those are big city boots."

Oooh.

So, I said it. "Those are my 'Yippee-I'm-finished-my-radiation boots! Boots like that *have* to be big; they *have* to be over the top; they *have* to be completely inappropriate."

Yes they do.

A couple of weeks later, Anna was getting dressed so that we could take Nathan to school in the morning. I never really monitor what she is wearing at this time, as I know she will change her outfit at least 17 times more before I take her to Kindergarten later in the day. But this day, I noticed her shoes.

"Um, Anna, I really like your shoes ..." —white, sparkly, ridiculously high-heeled sandals she received from a cousin—"but you can't wear them this morning ... in the snow."

"But Mummy," she shrieked at a decibel level indecent for that time of morning, "I *have* to wear these shoes. They are my 'Yippee-my-Mummy-is-finished-her-radiation shoes!'"

Case closed.

A very sweet story, but I can't help mourning the fact that my five-year-old daughter knows words like "radiation" and uses them in reference to her mother. It isn't right. A couple of days ago, she said, "Mummy, the *next* time you have cancer, we'll have to make sure we go to Victoria again." Ouch. The next time.

Last week, when she developed a cold, she ran from me shrieking and crying. When I tried to crawl into bed with her to snuggle her the way I always do when she is sick, she burst into tears and sobbed until I left the room. She didn't want me to catch her cold before I started chemo. *She* wanted to protect *me*.

Sigh.

February 5, 2008

A Long Day

Before she approached me, she robed herself in a hazardous material gown, and gloved her hands. The chemo is very harsh, and it burns skin on contact: and this is what she was about to pump into my body. These chemicals are designed to rid my body of the lingering cancer cells floating about, seeking a home in one of my organs, and I know in my head that because of this, they are "good" chemicals, and it's okay to let them in. But I couldn't help tensing up a little. At 10:30 a.m. it had already been a long day.

The day began early: I had to be at the hospital by 8:20 to get signed in, and get to my doctor's appointment by 8:30. We rushed around in the morning, packing lunches, having showers, issuing terse reminders and directions at each other. I was terser than anyone: miserable, bossy, cranky and irritable. I tried to stop barking orders, and making rude, impatient comments, but I was like a woman possessed. I had thought I was okay, that I had worked through my anxiety, but it certainly came out when I was bumped, or thwarted that morning. Ugly.

When my doctor walked into the room, I sighed a tiny inward sigh: young, blond, and beautiful. Oh well. She weighed me (sigh), checked my pulse, blood pressure, and the like, then she sat down to talk. We went over the whole story: last September seems like eons ago, and not mere months. I found I could hardly remember the surgery that had once loomed so large on my horizon.

Then I had to wait for about an hour, while the pharmacy got my drugs together. The nurse gave me a handful of meds to get me through the morning: a killer anti-nausea pill and two steroids.

"These are the ones that will make you want to go home and vacuum your entire house," she reminded me.

"But, I don't want to go home and vacuum my entire house. I want to go home and recline on my couch and watch very sad movies."

She laughed, and handed me the pills. I took them. I had come by myself, because I had thought I was feeling pretty brave, but found that I wasn't really so brave after all. Tears prickled behind my eyes, and I wandered down the hallway to find Dawn. "Maybe she will give me a hug," I thought. I really needed someone to touch me, and remind me that I was not alone, and that I would get through this. To quote Shakespeare, "Though she be little, yet she is fierce." That's Dawn, and I knew a hug from her would set me up for the day. I was right. Her eyes filled with compassion, she hugged me to her, and I felt her strength in me. Thank God for friends.

I walked down to the cafeteria and ate a tasteless muffin, and drank a cup of even more tasteless coffee. I listened to Mozart, and read Antony and Cleopatra.

I returned to the "chemo lounge" to have my cocktail. But before we could begin, the nurse had to make sure that the PICC line was working properly. It wasn't. She was able to inject the saline solution, but she wasn't able to draw it out again. This means that the line might not be in the vein, but in the tissue, and that is not good—it has to be in the vein, in order for the chemo to travel to where it needs to go. She had me standing up, flapping my arms, and doing various antics to make the saline draw out. But it wouldn't. Poor woman. Her day had been even longer than mine already, and so many things had gone wrong for her. And she is so patient, and so compassionate.

And so worried about me.

She was just saying that maybe they would have to take the line out and start again, when I felt the hairs on my arm standing on end and my lips start to tremble. I *was* brave, but this seemed a little beyond the pale. I gritted my teeth, and looked toward the door just in time to see Laurie walk in. I cannot say what relief flooded my being. She didn't need to say a word, or receive any explanation: with one glance at my face, she knew I was in distress, so she quietly hurried over, and took my hand in hers.

"Oh, I'm so glad you're here," said the nurse.

"Me too," I whispered.

I don't like things going wrong. I'm not a very flexible person, and I don't like the unknown.

"I have to go get the doctor," and the nurse hurried from the room.

"F***!" I whispered to Laurie.

Yes," she said. Sometimes no other word will do.

I looked up to see the doctor walk into the room: a lovely big man with twinkly eyes and a rueful smile. I love my doctors: they are all so sweet, kind, compassionate and good.

God has blessed me with health care professionals I respect and trust.

He checked out the line, and ordered a chest x-ray to make sure the line was where they wanted it to be. So, Laurie and I packed up and walked down to the imaging area—an area so packed with tired, irritated people that there were no seats. We waited in the hall. My name was called fairly quickly, and I got changed: "Everything off from the waist up," he said. And then he left me. I changed quickly, and was left standing awkwardly in the hall, waiting for him to come back.

I saw a woman I know slightly, and wanted to greet her, but felt so awkward and weird.

Would she remember me? Would she care if I said, "Hi"? Would she be annoyed at being interrupted at work? Why am I so weird? Why do I have to think so much, and worry even more? Why does it have to be all about me, and how I'm feeling?

Sometimes I think God must despair of me.

I had the x-ray, and got the go-ahead. Everything was in the right place, and we could proceed. So, we trudged back upstairs, and started all over. By this time, I was feeling really jittery and fragile. So, when the nurse donned her white gown, and approached me, I was a bit of a mess. I was so glad to have Laurie beside me, holding my hand. I was so glad to be loved.

And then everything was fine. Just long. It took another four hours to complete the treatment. I sent Laurie off to have lunch, and settled down to a nice hospital meal (the less said about that, the better.) I read my book, dozed in my chair, and listened to Pavarotti. The woman across from me had no occupation: no music, no book, no writing material, no handiwork. As Colonel Brandon says to Ellena at Marianne's sick bed, "I must have an occupation, or I shall go mad."

By 2:30, it was all over. I rose to my feet, a little unsteadily, and Laurie drove me to Bryan at school. It all seemed a little anti-climactic. But mercifully it is over. I have a little pump with me for the third medication: it will work for the next couple of days, and then I'll have to go in and have it disconnected. I have a hundred dollars' worth of meds to take home, and Bob's your uncle. One down, seven to go.

Light and Momentary Troubles

Bryan says that last week the ten plagues of Egypt assaulted his wife. I do not think it was that severe, but I do understand what he was getting at. On Monday, I had my first round of chemo; by Wednesday I was a quivering mass of nausea and fatigue. I tried to quit the dexamethasone so I could enjoy more than two hours of sleep at night. Mental note: do not try to quit the dexamethasone. Or, try to find something that will provide a similar energy boost, so that you can do your day—you know, get dressed, feed the family, drive a car. I stopped by Shan's house on Wednesday, because I needed to rest and didn't think I could drive home. Within minutes, I was sound asleep on her couch, oblivious to the noise of her two small children, and the muffled sounds of chores being done. Really. When I came to, more than 40 minutes had passed. On Friday, the plague of diarrhea struck; Saturday, mouth sores; Sunday, irritated and peeling skin on the soles of my feet. Pleasant.

Yesterday I had a follow-up appointment in Victoria with my notorious radiation oncologist: the man with the emotional range of a two-by-four. Bryan and I had a lovely drive down, unmarred by arguments, tears, whining or complaints (we had left the kids behind). We talked, listened to music, read, listened to CBC radio—we *love* road trips (or used to BC–before children.) But as soon as the car turned up Hillside, heading towards the Cancer Clinic, my stomach clenched with nausea. I guess it was the association of ideas: leaving home and loved ones, enduring rounds of treatments that ravaged my body and my spirit, living uneasily among strangers. It was very disconcerting.

And then Dr. A. On my last day of treatments, I had heard from my radiation therapist that Dr. A. is a great guy—very funny, and very entertaining. A guy you would like to hang out with at the bar. A guy you would catch on film doing slightly embarrassing things at the staff Christmas party, and then perhaps use those photos for a bit of blackmail afterwards. That's what she said, as I sat before her, wondering if there could be two radiation oncologists of the same name in the Victoria Cancer Clinic. Maybe I had misjudged the man.

So, he strolled into the room and asked about three questions concerning my recovery from radiation. I answered, briefly. After about three minutes, he made motions as if he was going to rise and leave. I thought to myself, "I did *not* just drive three hours, to have a three-minute appointment!" And I thought of a couple of questions to ask. He answered, briefly.

"I think I've started menopause," I said. "That'll give him pause to think," I thought.

"Well, you might want to start some hormone replacement," he said. "You're still *pretty* young."

"Hmpf," I thought.

"How old are you, anyway?"

"Forty-four," I replied, stiffly.

"Tuh, well, you would have started soon, anyway, so it *probably doesn't really matter.*" (Emphasis mine, of course.)

Nice. A far cry from my lovely, darling surgeon, who said, "I made the smallest incision possible on your abdomen because you are still *so young* and so active." He has such beautiful manners.

I just need to say that *it does matter!!!* It matters because my body has been completely and irrevocably changed. I *know* the change would have happened sooner or later: it's not the inevitability that bothers me, it's the precipitous-ness that galls me. It's the fact that it's another change foisted upon me by this disease. It's the fact that my body wasn't allowed to come to its natural fruition. It's the night sweats and sleeplessness on top of all the other side effects from the chemo.

It's the loss of youth. My fruitfulness was so short-lived, that it's a bit hard to say goodbye to it already. Silly, I know, but there it is.

And I might not have minded so much, were it not for a callous doctor treating me and my ovaries with such a cavalier attitude.

The doctor who inserted my PICC line crouched on the floor at my knee, and tenderly asked, "And why do *you* need a PICC line?"

"Chemo," I replied.

His face crumpled into a sympathetic grimace. "I'm so sorry," he said. And he meant it.

Sweet man.

Maybe I'm just used to garnering sympathy. Cancer brings it out in even the most hardened people. Probably Dr. A. has seen too much to be concerned about one woman's premature menopause. I'm sure he has. Six weeks at that clinic brought me to my knees. One brief trip back almost undid me. Imagine working there.

I'd rather not.

I'll take the high road. I'll forgive Dr. A. I'll even stop whining. I'm not really *that* bothered by it all. It was just an odd moment. And it made me think too much as usual: too much about myself and my minor troubles. My "light and momentary troubles."

More on that later.

The Stress Ball

I wonder, in the midst of all this, why it's so hard to change. Why I still hold out, or hold back on God. Why my voice is mute, when I wish to speak. Why I can't give to Him what He wants me to give. Why I can't surrender all.

I keep thinking that I'm coming to the end of myself, that there can't be much more of me to slough off. I've already done some pretty serious shedding. In times like this, all sorts of things bubble up to the surface to confound us and confront us with who we really are and why we do what we do. It's not a pretty picture.

Someone told me once that people die in the same way that they lived; they don't change just because they are dying. That's a rather sobering thought. I don't want to die the way I lived. I want to be different. Newer. Better. Changed.

I wondered what cancer would do to me. I know now that it is not death: not now, anyway. But it is *big*. Life-altering. Daunting. Unknown and Unknowable. Somehow, when this all began, I thought I might change more quickly. More spectacularly. More measurably.

I *have* changed, but ever so slowly. And I wonder, when all this is over, if I will go back to who I was before. Like one of those stress balls. You squeeze it, and when you let go, it retains the new shape. You think it might stay that way, but within a few minutes it has slowly returned to its original shape. I don't want to return to my original shape.

Waiting has never been my strong suit, and so I want those sweeping changes now. I get so tired of that me-part that drags me down when I wish to soar. The filthy rotten me-part that sullies me when I wish to be clean. And yet, I know that Jesus died for that part, and that if it wasn't for that part, I wouldn't need a Saviour. I do need Him. And He loves me in spite of that me-part. Or because of it. Or something.

February 16, 2008

No Reservations

Last week, as I was resting on the couch, I had a bit of an epiphany.

I need my friends. I need them to hug me. To ask me how I'm feeling. To cook meals for me. To take care of my children. To pray for me. To encourage me. To touch me.

I need them; I depend on them. When I am weak and weary, I need them to enfold me in their arms and whisper my name. No other words are necessary. And when that happens, I feel buoyed up by their strength, bolstered by their love. My friends are fierce, and I need them.

I think I used to be afraid of that kind of weakness or neediness. I think maybe I put walls around myself, fooled myself into thinking I was strong. Pushed people away. Didn't need anyone.

I loved people, but I don't think I let them in: only so far, and no farther. I was guarded, protective, prideful: fiercely independent, like a child who brushes away a helping hand. I didn't know then that "I don't need help" is sometimes interpreted as "I don't need *you*."

I've always been really reluctant to ask for help; reluctant to admit that I couldn't do something myself; reluctant to admit my inadequacies.

Even when all this happened, I didn't want to ask for help. I didn't mind asking for prayer, but I didn't want to ask for help. Why? I think I felt I could manage on my own; that I didn't want to be a burden to my friends; that others were worse off than me, and *they* needed help. I've always been very good at being *needed*, but not so good at being *needy*.

I was talking to Tony (my homeopath) about this one day. He said that when I talked about someone offering me something, my whole body recoiled, and I drew my hands back ... and they were clenched into fists.

"Is this how you respond, when someone tries to give you something?" he asked.

"Yes," I whispered, "I think it is."

He merely nodded. And I knew then that I would have to take some time to re-examine this.

I have a friend whose elderly mother lives in a building with other elderly people, all living independently. Strangely, these people all see the age and infirmities of the other residents, but not their own. They will leap to their feet to help a friend with his groceries, muttering all the while, "What were you thinking? You can't possibly manage these groceries by yourself; they are far too heavy for you." And they snatch the bags from the other. The speaker might be a tiny, frail, 90-year-old woman who walks with a cane; the recipient of her attentions might be an 87-year-old man who uses a walker.

It seems to be a human condition that we can recognize the neediness of others, but not our own.

I said earlier that I always thought I could manage on my own. I wonder now if that might be the real disease that threatens me. Not cancer. Pride. Independence. A fierce and obsessive need for privacy. An urge to keep something of myself separate from the God who loves me, who holds me close in the darkness and sings over me like a father over His infant child.

That was the real sin of Adam and Eve. It wasn't the disobedience; it was that streak of independence that led them to act without reference to God and His design for their lives. They held out on God; they disregarded Him.

I think I've spent a great deal of time managing my life without God. Disregarding Him. "I can do it by myself," I say with grit-

---

ted teeth, not unlike my five-year-old daughter when she brush-es me away.

I know I needed Him for salvation. I admitted my deep need for Him then—all those years ago when I first knew that He loved me. He accomplished for me what I could never have accom-plished for myself. And there have been many times since then when I know I have needed him. But what I'm beginning to see is that I can't *manage* without Him: I want to be near Him ev-ery moment of every day, walking with Him, talking with Him, comparing notes, chatting, listening, laughing, loving, being.

And maybe that's why I am where I am today. God wants my heart. I want Him to have it; I've always yearned for that, but I've always been so consumed by my life that I have never fig-ured out how to give it. How to manage with Him, rather than without Him. How to let Him in completely, utterly, unreserv-edly. I've always known that more was possible, but I've never plumbed the depths of my neediness to find Him waiting there. I've never taken the time. But these days, that's all I have. Time.

"Take me to you; imprison me for I/ Except you enthrall me, never shall be free/ Nor ever chaste except you ravish me" (*Batter My Heart, Three-Person'd God*, John Donne).

I prayed for something the other day; I needed God to provide something for us. He answered within a couple of hours, but when it came, I didn't want to take it from the person who offered it. I felt badly about taking it. I had already accepted so much, and I didn't want to accept any more. How foolish is that? To ask for something, but not take it when it is proffered. Silly, but so typical of me and my dealings with God. When will I be able to accept that He delights in me and yearns to fulfill my needs? I need to open my hands to God: my hands and my heart.

In the same way, when a friend offers help, I need to reach out my open hands to receive the blessing; for if I refuse, I rob us both.

February 21, 2008

Just Have To Say

I feel so terrible, and if I don't write about it, I think I'll go crazy. I don't feel as nauseated as I did yesterday, but just as desperate and unhappy. My brain is so fuzzy; I can't concentrate; I can't think straight; my mind wanders; and all my thoughts are disjointed and unreal.

And I feel so alone.

I know I'm *not* alone, but I feel so alone. Last week, I remember thinking, "Chemo is not so hard ... I can do this."

What was I thinking?

This is really hard.

I know, now, that it will get better as the week progresses; that by Saturday, I will have returned to myself again. But that doesn't help me much today.

Two down; six to go. On Monday, that seemed a happy thought—that I was making progress, getting somewhere. Today, I find no comfort in that thought. Today, I can't believe that I can do this *six* more times; that I will *choose* to do this again.

But, I will.

I want to be so brave and strong, but I just can't. I don't have it in me. I'm weak, and unhappy, and miserable, and tired.

On Sunday, Randy said that when people are ill and worn down, they can't pray for themselves. It's true. I can't even pray today; all I can do is cry out wordlessly, and hope He hears.

Oddly, now that I have splatted all that out, and have dried my tears, I feel a sense of release. I'm a little better—as if all that despair was a part of the problem.

I *will* be better.

This will *not* last forever.

Having just received an incoherent phone call from her hysterical friend, Elvera is now praying for me ... and God really *loves* Elvera, so I know He is listening.

He loves me, too—so I know He is listening.

February 27, 2008

Another Paradox

Feeling so much better today than I did a week ago. That was a tough round, but I think I have at least learned my lesson: I really must take the extra meds to help me through the really hard days just after my treatment. So many people have told me that you really can't let things gets away from you—you may feel fine, but if you don't take the meds, you crash. So true. On Tuesday, I felt pretty well, so thought I could get along fine on my own. Big mistake. By Wednesday, the fatigue was so debilitating, I could not function; and along with that came depression and despair. Silly to think that taking the meds is somehow a sign of weakness; that somehow I should be able to deal with the toxins in my body without any help. But in all fairness, it is also the fact that the extra meds bring all sorts of other issues along with them, and I would like to give my kidneys and other organs a bit of a break. However, the *most* important thing is that I be able to function at some level of normalcy for the sake of my family: it certainly doesn't do my children any good to see their mother in such a state as I was in last week.

I think I also have to reconcile myself to the fact that I will not *really* feel well again until well after the last chemo treatment. The first round had gone so well that I thought it would continue to be fairly easy. But in this round, I have been so disappointed that my so-called "good" week really hasn't been so good. I tire so easily, and I have fewer reserves than I thought I did. And it's so frustrating when I think I have enough energy to complete a certain task, only to find myself trembling and clammy, and in dire need of a nap halfway through the job. Or, to realize that I *might* have the wherewithal to make dinner, or do the laundry, or play for a short time with my children, but not enough to do it all. I really *do* need to pace myself, to choose carefully how I expend myself, to be more self-aware than I have been.

And this, too, is difficult. For this entire year, I have spent so much time on myself: so much time caring for my own needs, thinking of what is best for me, limiting my focus to me and my family. I feel as though I have been living this year in a close-up, rather than in a wide angle shot, and it makes me feel uncomfortable and self-centred: useless, ineffectual, and unloving. I know the world has gone on for my friends and acquaintances, but for me it has seemed to stand still, and I know that I haven't met my friends in their needs and sorrows, that I haven't been able to be the friend I would like to have been. That grieves me, even though I know they understand.

Many people have told me that this year is all about me; that it *has* to be all about me, so that I can get better, and move forward with life. Ouch. I don't like that thought—it grates on my nerves, and makes me very uncomfortable. But, at the same time, it has made me really look at myself and determine what makes me happy. Someone asked me a few weeks ago if my needs are being met. I paused for a long time, not knowing how to respond. I said, "I think so." He said, "Well, what *are* your needs?" I paused even longer, and then said, "I need to look after my family, I need to rest, I need to be alone." Taking care of my family gives me a sense of peace and fulfillment: resting restores my energy; being alone restores my sense of balance, and helps me understand who I am and how I am growing through this mess. But it doesn't leave a lot of room for anyone else. And so this year has been one in which my horizons have at once expanded and diminished.

Another paradox.

March 6, 2008

Lashed by Storms

A friend of ours died in the night: we heard the news on Monday morning. We didn't know her well, but we loved her. Her daughter, in Nathan's class at school, is eight years old.

Anna (who is five) said to me, "Mummy, I am *so* tired of people getting sick and dying."

"I am, too, my darling," I answered.

She stood in front of me with her arms crossed and her foot tapping impatiently, "And I am *so* disappointed that this is what God planned."

Gulp.

"Me too," I whispered. And I crouched down, put my arms around her and held her close. "But there are two things I know, my child: I trust God, and I know that He loved Sherri more than anyone else in her life ever could. She is home with Him."

And it's true. I am finding it very hard to be sad for Sherri. She had a very hard life, full of physical pain and infirmity, and emotional turmoil. Even though she had a beautiful daughter, and a sweet, loving husband, the burdens of her heart were momentous, and every day was a struggle.

But now, she is free. Free from the physical pain; free from the emotional anguish; free to love and be loved. Completely unfettered from this jar of clay, this weak vessel that cracks at the least provocation, Sherri is now able to know the love of God perfectly, intimately, purely. The tears of all her sorrows have been dried, and she is whole.

But in the hallway at school, I pass a child without a mother, a husband without a wife, a mother without her daughter, and my heart clenches within me. I grieve for them: for their empty arms, for their weeping hearts, for their confusion and sorrow and distress.

And, like Anna, I am disappointed that this is the plan. That the price of Sherri's freedom and consolation is sorrow for all who held her dear. I am disappointed that Katelyn faces a lifetime without her mother, and Steve face a future without his wife. And yet, I say again that I trust God, and I have to hope that this plan will work out for good, somehow. That God will bring healing and wholeness and a return to life for them. That they will laugh again, and find joy despite the pain that will from this moment on be the constant companion of their hearts.

> O, Afflicted One, lashed by
> storms and not comforted,
> I will build you with stones of
> Turquoise,
> foundations with
> with sapphires.
> I will make your battlements
> of rubies,
> your gates of sparkling
> jewels,
> and all your walls of precious stones.
> All your sons will be taught
> by the Lord.
> And great will be your
> children's peace
> In righteousness you will be
> established.
> Tyranny will be far from you;
> you have nothing to fear.

Isaiah 54

March 12, 2008
May 12th

I had a terrible cold last week: really terrible. Raw, irritated throat, congested sinuses, racking cough. Argh. All I could think was, "Nuts! This is supposed to be my 'good' week. I'm supposed to feel well, have energy, be happy." I was none of the above.

Went in on Tuesday to have my dressing changed, and to see if I could have my treatment on Wednesday. The nurse thought it would be okay. Then I asked if this would put me off schedule, or if I would be able to get on track again.

"On track?" she asked blankly.

"Yeah," I said, "I'm just wondering if I'll be able to have my next treatment on schedule."

"On schedule?" she asked.

I was beginning to wonder which of us had a problem.

"You're not putting dates on your calendar, are you?" she asked.

"Um," I faltered.

"You're not circling dates of treatments, are you? You don't have an end date marked in red ink, do you?" she demanded, vehemently.

"Um ..."

"Because *there are no dates!* Remember, I told you the first day we met, that you *do not put dates on your calendar!*"

I did not remember. I had all my dates circled in red. May 12th circled several times, with little stars and happy faces around it.

"*No dates!*" she reiterated, and I left.

The next day, when I was sitting in the chemo lounge having my cocktail, the nurse said to the other patient, "Denise, you need to tell Sandy about dates, and why we never circle anything on the calendar."

So, Denise told me about the day her white blood count plunged to zero and her treatments were suspended for an entire month.

Sigh. And I was worried about a two-day delay.

Lord, preserve me. I say now that I couldn't stand it ... but I could. Of course I could, if I had to.

But I hope I don't have to.

I didn't erase the happy faces. Or the circle.

May 12th.

March 12, 2008

Away from Myself

I'm back. Suddenly at seven o'clock last night, I sat up in my bed and thought, "Oh. I'm better." And that was weird, because I had been gone for so long, I wondered if I would be able to return at all this time.

When I have chemo, I feel as though part of me packs up and moves away for a few days. I don't know where I go, or how I'll get back, but I know that part of me is gone.

It's like I become one of those hollow chocolate Easter bunnies: part of the ears and feet are delicious solid chunks of creamy chocolate, but the middle is completely hollow and unsatisfying. A travesty.

I cannot shake the feeling of unreality. I cannot clear my head.

Four or five days of dying, ever so slowly. I can almost feel myself leave. The first day or two after the treatment are pretty good—I feel only a slight lassitude. But the third hits hard, and I wake up knowing that I'm gone, and wondering when I'll be back. I can't focus my thoughts; my emotions run rampant; I feel detached from everyone I hold dear. I feel that I have to work really hard to hold myself together, that I have to hold myself really tightly, or I might fly apart and never come together again; my jaw aches with the clenching. My thoughts are dreamlike and unreal; when I speak, I can never be sure if what I say will make any sense to anyone. I crave solitude, but I hate to be alone. When I'm out in public, I'm afraid to look people in the eye, because I might have to talk to them, and I have no energy to talk, no desire to be dragged into the pool of humanity, no ability to relate to anyone.

I fall away, and I can't claw my way back.

But, miraculously, a few days later I have a rebirth of sorts. I'm a new person, with hope, and happiness,and a future beyond my bedroom walls. I laugh, and talk and embrace life again.

I lead a double life.

March 23, 2008

The Zipper

About twelve years ago, my brother shamed me into going on a terrifying ride when the carnival came to town. I like huge roller coasters, and thrill rides, but I've never been fond of rides that shake you until your teeth ache, and spin you so fast you don't know which way is up. So, I'm not really sure how he got me on The Zipper; but as soon as the ride began, I knew I had made a terrible mistake. The cage I was in tipped upside-down and spun slowly up as the next cage was boarded; this continued until all the cages were full, and all the while, I gritted my teeth and tried to keep a leash on my rising panic. And then the ride began in earnest. I can't really even explain how it felt except to say that at some point I remember thinking, "This must be what Hell feels like." A roaring filled my ears, my body was jarred in every direction, with no predictable pattern, so there was no way of bracing myself for the next onslaught; I was disoriented, confused and panicked. When I left the ride, my legs wobbled, my stomach churned, and I needed to spend the next few hours in bed with the curtains closed against the bright light of day. It was a hideous experience.

In some strange way, the days immediately following my chemo remind me of that ride. Obviously my body is not being physically tossed around as it was on The Zipper, but my spirit faces a similar assault. I have no peace of mind for several days: no rest. My body curls up, exhausted, on my bed while my mind spins out of control. A vast roaring fills my senses, and I cannot concentrate on any thought except, "Please make this stop. I want it to be over."

I went to church on Good Friday; it was probably a mistake. I was too raw to be in public. Someone spoke to me, and it seemed to me as though I had to reign in my mind from the farthest reaches. I could hardly move my lips to give the answers to his questions, and I felt I was in grave danger of saying something that might be deemed very inappropriate for a church foyer, or just inappropriate for the question asked. I felt I couldn't trust myself to speak.

We sat down, and I saw a friend I hadn't seen for a few days. I wondered why she was at church, because I knew that she had plans to go away for the first part of Spring Break. I sat there, mulling it over, and wondering if I should ask her why she hadn't gone away, when I came to the muddled realization that the first part of Spring Break was over. I turned to Bryan, and said through stiff lips, "Did we have a whole week of Spring Break, and I missed it?" His eyes filled with tears, and he nodded. "I guess I went away for a week, didn't I?" He nodded, again. "Well, I just want you to know that I didn't have any *fun* while I was gone!"

I'm sort of aghast to realize that those days are gone, and I have hardly any recollection of them. To me, they are a blur of restless tossing, and roaring in my ears, and spinning thoughts that reeled me into the darkness. No peace, and hardly any awareness that peace exists somewhere.

I remember wishing that everyone I know could take turns coming over to my house and holding me in their arms, so that I could know I wasn't alone. I needed a strong, physical reassurance that I was still here, and that I was going to make it back again.

And then I remembered God. Why is it sometimes so hard for me to remember God? I may feel that I am spinning out of control, and heading into the darkness of the abyss, but He is cradling me, and holding me close.

He reached down from on high and took hold of me;
he drew me out of deep waters.
He rescued me from my powerful enemy,

from my foes who were too strong for me.
They confronted me in the day of my disaster,
but the Lord was my support.
He brought me out into a spacious place;
he rescued me because he delighted in me."

Psalm 18:16-19

I do not know, or understand how it is possible for the Lord of All to find *any* delight in me, but I find so much comfort in the thought that He does. He loves me, and when the cords of death entangle me, and the torrents of destruction overwhelm me, I can cry to my God for help.

And He hears my voice.

April 5, 2008

Three Left

I haven't written for a long time. My latest round of chemo went better than the last, and five days later, I am shaky and tremulous, but not in despair.

Friday, as usual, was a difficult day—replete with desolation and intestinal cramping—but it is over, and there are only three more Fridays to face.

Three more. People are always trying to encourage me by reminding me how the treatments are passing, and how few I have left.

I have a hard time seeing that. When I'm in the midst of my fog, I can see nothing beyond the moment, and even thinking of facing *one* more treatment is enough to reduce me to a quivering mound of goo. It's hard to imagine feeling well again, and not dreading the future.

I do dread it. Every second Monday gets harder and harder to face. I want to be calm and serene, but I can't manage it. Last Monday I cried all the way home. It's not that I was feeling that badly, it's just that I have no barriers left, and every emotion is raw and untutored. No reserves.

And yet ... I don't think I would turn back the clock. If given the chance to change the past, I don't think I would.

In spite of the sorrow, and discomfort, and dread—or perhaps *because* of it—my life is sweet. Every day, or almost every day, contains some flash of incandescence. Beauty, truth, kindness, generosity and goodness flash out "like shook foil."

A few examples from just this week:

- a lovely supper delivered to my home every second Tuesday by my kind, loving, generous friend, who has a full life of her own, and yet finds the time to care for us in such a practical way. This week supper was accompanied by a beautiful basket of spring flowers whose scent made me believe that Spring would come to me again.

- a gorgeous bunch of luscious, velvety red roses hand-delivered to my home by my doctor—a woman who loves me and prays for me every day.

- a lavish and sumptuous pizza feast made by a co-worker—a huge delight to my hungry children.

- a basket stuffed full lovely of fruit, cards and gifts from two women I hardly know. We attend the same church, and they have been praying for me and my family throughout the year, and wanted to encourage me with these tokens of their love and encouragement. Their hugs strangled me, and I felt so humbled by their regard.

- coffee out with a friend. On Friday. In the middle of my fuzz and fog. She loves me. And even though I could barely carry on a conversation, she thanked me for listening. It made me feel real again.

These are only a few examples of the blessings that have come my way this week. But my hands are shaking, and my thoughts are beginning to blur.

I don't write as often as I used to. Part of that is because my weeks are relentlessly similar: stretches of recovery smattered with days of laughter and hope.

Laughter and hope. And sometimes, the knowledge that one day I'll be well again.

April 12, 2008

To Sleep, Perchance to Dream

I'm having the strangest dreams. I almost dread going to sleep for fear of what my unconscious will drag up.

Dream 1

I'm in the downtown east-side at a so-called "safe house" for families. I walk in, and the place is crowded with unkempt, bristly-faced men sporting torn white T-shirts. As I approach, one man starts complaining about his wife. He says that the moment he walks in the door after work, his wife abdicates responsibility for the kids, and expects him to "baby-sit" (He does not, of course, use polysyllabic words like "abdicate" or "responsibility" but he does use an impressive array of curse words.) He begins hurling abuse at me, and is soon joined by all the other men at the Centre who all know my failings and shortcomings. Apparently the "safe- house" is a safe place for the men, and not for me. I leave, feeling like a loser.

As I walk down the street, I encounter a woman who begins to harangue me for my failure to address the issue of the prostitutes who have disappeared from the downtown east-side. She accuses me of being lazy, selfish and ignorant. I know she is right, and I try to flee, but she chases me, hurling abuse at the top of her voice.

I wake up exhausted.

Dream 2

I am in a field in Black Creek. I have been planting this field every spring for years, but I have never reaped a harvest. Somehow, every fall, a thief steals the crop, and I have never been able to stop him. My family is starving. And now, to top it all off, the soil is now ruined—it is thick, heavy and infertile. As

I contemplate what to do, a young bull approaches. I am lactating, and for some reason, that seems to annoy the bull. He charges me. I know that if he touches me, I will die. I escape by climbing a tree.

I wake up, exhausted.

Dream 3

I have to walk to Nunavut. I trudge along in the snow for months, but I can never reach my destination. I am cold, tired and discouraged. Every time I think I am getting somewhere, the scene shifts, and I am lost. I waste time retracing my steps, and finding my path again.

I wake up, exhausted, having never reached my destination.

After two years of seeing my homeopath, I am a little better at finding meaning in my dreams. I dream often and vividly; however, during my illness I have remembered very few dreams. These three dreams are pretty clear indicators of my current state of mind.

The first dream reflects what is happening in my family. My son has had a very difficult week. When people ask me how my children are doing, I tend to respond pretty positively. My children seem to be coping well. But this week has shown me that it's all smoke and mirrors. Because with kids, you don't really know how it's going, until it isn't going at all ... and that's when the s*** hits the fan. Nathan fell apart this week: behaviour problems at school, rudeness at home, tears, reproaches, fears—a lot of fears that we had never seen before. Fear of fire, fear of strangers, fear of separation, fear of haircuts, fear of being looked at, fear of being the centre of attention. After a particularly difficult day, he burst into heaving sobs, and cast himself on my bosom. I felt helpless, and yet I suddenly understood. "Nathan, do you think all this is really about me? About you being afraid that I am going to die? You see me sick and weak in bed, and you worry that I am not going to get better?"

"Yes," he managed to choke out.

I am aghast at my obtuseness.

I see that I *have* abdicated responsibility, in so many ways. I *have* expected my husband to gather up the reins and do everything around the house. I *have* turned a blind eye to suffering *in my own home!* I see that I am not the only one who is desolate and alone, afraid and unable to fully articulate it.

The second dream is a little harder to pin down. I think it has something to do with my feelings of futility over my treatments. I keep going for the treatments, but I don't see any progress: not unlike planting a crop, but never reaping a harvest. The chemo "thief" robs me, but I can never bring him to justice, so he "gets away with it." My family is starved for my attention, because no matter how "good" my day is, it's not really very good, and no matter how well I am feeling, it's always relative. I feel better than I did last week—but since last week I was curled up in a little ball on bed, it's not a very good measure. I may be able to play for ten minutes, but my daughter really wants me to play for an hour. Last week, after a pathetic attempt to play Polly Pockets for ten minutes, and then being too exhausted to even be the voices while Anna acted out the action, she folded her arms and said, "Mummy, I wish you never got that cancer."

Yeah: you and me both, Baby.

The heavy, infertile soil of the dream is my ruined, infertile body. No matter how much fertilizer I fold into it, it's never going to bear fruit again.

The meaning of the lactating part eludes me.

The bull is cancer.

The third dream is painfully obvious. The trek to Nunavut is my journey towards wellness. I've been trudging for months, and sometimes despair that I will ever reach my destination. I wander in the dark fog of chemotherapy, seeking out the right path and trying to find my way. Why I would be going to Nunavut and not somewhere warm is beyond me. Perhaps Nunavut represents the farthest place a person can go without falling into the sea. Perhaps it is farther that I can imagine.

Perhaps it is unattainable.

Last night I dreamed I was shopping for the right bra. Every time I awoke, I went to sleep again right back into the same dream. I must have tried on a hundred bras from dozens of different stores, but I never found one that fit properly.

Again that motif of searching for something that proves to be elusive.

I wonder. I wonder if it will prove to be elusive, or if one day I'll find it.

I wonder if the destination will be found, or if I will wander in the wilderness forever.

I wonder if I'll live up to my responsibilities again, or if I'll continue to slough them off on others.

But most of all I wonder why I was lactating in that dream, and why it infuriated the bull so powerfully.

April 15, 2008

A Bag of Gold

Yesterday afternoon as I sat in the sun, I had an epiphany.

Since my cancer was first diagnosed on August 31, I've been able to see the power and beauty and truth of my experiences throughout this long and arduous journey: the flashes of incandescence I wrote about a couple of weeks ago. Sickness, suffering, anxiety and fear have new faces, new sweetness that I was never able to see until they became the constant companions of my nights. I knew that my suffering was achieving for me a new perspective, a more refined character, a deeper joy. And I even described this year as a gift. But what I didn't realize until yesterday is that it's not the year that's the gift. It's the cancer. The cancer is the bag of gold dropped into my lap to enrich my life.

It's almost as if those dreams I had last week brought the last of my dread to the surface to dissipate in the light of day, freeing me to embrace the rest of my treatment rather than flinching from it and teaching me to feel enriched by the cancer rather than robbed by it.

I'm still reeling with the wonder of it all.

And it might not make sense to anyone but me.

And it might be the deranged ponderings of a chemo-fried brain.

But it might be the truth. And it might help me make it through the last few weeks of my treatments, because now I think I might be able to walk up the stairs of the hospital without a clenching dread gnawing at my heart. And on the days when I am away from myself, I might be able to rest instead of fight. I might be able to surrender myself to the befuddlement rather than struggle for clarity and control. Maybe this is the last front in my war for control. Maybe this is where I finally lay down my arms and sign for peace. Or maybe it's just another skirmish.

In any case, today I felt lighter than I have in weeks. On the weekend, I caught my PICC on something and ripped it out partway. Today I had to have it fixed, and I couldn't have my treatment. I'll have it tomorrow. When I went into the chemo room today, I had laughter on my lips. When I saw the doctor who was going to fix my PICC, I laughed again. He asked if I was worried about the procedure this time, and I realized I wasn't. Even when he had difficulty doing what he wanted to do, I didn't worry—I prayed. And I hadn't been able to do that in the hospital for quite some time.

So hooray for bad dreams. Let me correct myself. Tony would say that it was not a "bad" dream; it was a dream that revealed something important. So hooray for revealing dreams. Hooray for truth and beauty.

Hooray for cancer.

Near the End

I had my treatment last Monday: the sixth of eight treatments. I felt so much more at peace: as if I had finally resigned myself, after so long, to the onslaught against my body. I did not cry all the way home. In fact, I did not go home at all: I saw my surgeon, I sat by the ocean, I picked my children up from school.

I held that image of the worn leather bag and the treasure within as consciously as I could, and when the crash came, as it always does, I held it even closer. I slept more this time, and I didn't feel as desolate and alone. I think I was able to surrender myself and find solace in sleep, rather than struggle against the tide of confusion. I slept for almost twenty-four hours, but still woke on Saturday, exhausted.

On Sunday I tried to go to church. Mistake. I love to go to church now, and worship with my friends, and sing and pray and be with the people I love. But on Sunday it was a mistake: I wasn't well enough—too shaky, too exhausted, too dizzy. I had to make a rather ignominious retreat. And I cried all the way home. And I frightened my children. And Nathan got sick. And Anna's eyes were the size of dinner plates.

In between my wails, I heard Nathan's voice from the back seat, "They say that laughter is contagious ... I think sadness is contagious too."

Oh, my children.

Sometimes the burden of grief is too much to bear, and it spills out, and I can't stop it, and I don't even know if I even should stop it. And my children see it, and soak it up, and store it up in their little hearts, and I wonder what it will create in them. What will be their prevailing memories of this year? How will it change them? How *has* it changed them? I don't want to deny the pain, brush it away, and pretend it doesn't exist, but I don't want it to become the constant refrain of our home, either.

I have cried in front of my children many times: gentle, oozy tears. My emotions have always run close to the surface. But I don't often sob uncontrollably in front of them.

So Nathan has been home all week with the dreadful wracking cough he develops when he is under stress. He has had it three times this year: when I had my surgery, when I was in treatment in Victoria, and now. He comes for snuggles twenty times a day. He is teary and fragile. It's funny how children differ: Nathan becomes fragile; Anna becomes demanding. She is the imperious princess who demands attention. She wants to play, she needs a snack, she can't find her favourite dress, she wants to go for a walk, she needs a snuggle. Arghh. And my patience is so thin, I hear it in my voice: stretched taut and querulous.

So, even though I was able to surrender to the experience this time, and find a measure of solace and peace, I don't think my children were able to do so. I don't know whether it is possible for them to do so: their mother is so paramount to their world that seeing her sick or in pain is earth-shaking. Even today, I feel my world quake when I see tears in my mother's eyes, or hear a tremble in her voice when we speak on the phone: a cold rush of dread fills me when I think of my mother sick, in pain ... dying. And I am 44 years old!!!! How much more for my little ones, whose mother is so present and so needful for their comfort.

I don't really know why I'm writing all this. When I began, I thought this post would be positive, happy—would reveal my sense of relief at seeing a glimpse of the end. But then the events of the week pressed against me, and I saw a more realistic picture of the week that was. I couldn't see it before—I wasn't really present.

Yesterday morning Nathan woke early, came for a snuggle, and was finally able to articulate some of his fears and anxieties. I'm so grateful for Chris and Laurie, who have modeled to us for so many years how to parent effectively, how to listen to children, how to care for their hearts. I never would have known how to wait for my son to be ready, or how to draw him out, and read his silences. I wouldn't have known how to live in the hard places without having watched them live there and seen how to do it. I didn't know before how to walk through the pain: in my family, we pretended it wasn't there.

When I look at my life from this vantage point, I see so clearly how God has orchestrated the details to bring me to where I am today. Chris and Laurie have mentored us in almost every aspect of our lives. They were parents in a time when we thought we would never have children of our own, and they welcomed us into their family, and gave us the joy and privilege of sharing in their children's lives. We learned how to be parents by watching them.

In fact, we've watched Chris and Laurie walk through all sorts of life experiences: mental and emotional breakdowns, the terminal illness of a parent, church issues, death, relationships, past pain, present sufferings, you name it, they've been there. And what I've learned most from them is how to live *in* the pain, even *rest* in the pain and *not* flee from it.

God brought me to this place at this time with life lessons I've seen in Chris and Laurie. They are not perfect. They make mistakes. But they have had a powerful impact on me and my family, and I am so thankful, and sort of awed that God worked it all out. And what is even more cool is how their children are carrying on the legacy with my children. Luke, Sarah and Fergie have mentored my children and loved them so utterly in all of this. They have cared for them like siblings, and my children have flourished under their care.

God really loves us.

April 26, 2008

So Much Depends

Anna: Mummy, I think it would be good if Daddy married another wife and I could have *two* mummies.

Me: Two mummies? Why would you want to have two mummies?

Anna: You could be the mummy *with* cancer, and you could stay in bed all day, and not do any work. Then I could have a mummy *without* cancer, and she could do the dishes and the laundry and play with me.

Me: I'd rather be the mummy without cancer.

A couple of days ago I really needed to be alone. By the ocean. In the sun. Nathan had been home sick all week, and it had been a very difficult couple of days: stressful, listening to his cough, and feeling like it was my fault he was sick. And I needed to be alone, to think, and to wonder.

Now that I can begin to see the end of all things, I've begun to wonder again. What about the future? What about the cancer? While I was having chemo the other day, I picked up a book from the shelf behind me: The Complete Guide to Colorectal Cancer. I flipped to the chapter entitled "Life after Cancer." The first thing I read was rather startling: it turns out that there isn't any—life after cancer, that is. Some sort of freaky, scary statistic leapt out at me: even after five years cancer-free, many people still succumb to colorectal cancer. I closed the book, put it back on the shelf. "I don't think I can read this right now," I whispered to Laurie. She nodded.

But on Thursday, when I had my dressing changed, I decided that I *did* need to read it. I've done pitifully little reading about this disease, and I need to know a few things. But this time I picked up a different book: *The Intelligent Patient Guide to Colorectal Cancer*. Not that I am—intelligent, that is—I just hoped it might have a different statistic, a different take on the future.

Here are some things I read. Let me note that the sun was no longer shining down by the ocean. An icy wind had blown up, and dark rain clouds threatened overhead. In fiction, it is a device known as pathetic fallacy, whereby the events in nature reflect the happenings in the plot.

- 1 in 15 Canadians will get colorectal cancer at some point in their lifetime, and 1 in 28 will die of it.

- Patients who have had one colorectal cancer are at increased risk of developing another one.

- Colorectal cancer will recur in 50% of patients who have been treated.

- If a colon or rectal cancer is going to recur, either locally (in the area of the original cancer) or as a metastases elsewhere in the body, most often it will do so in the first two years after surgery.

- More than 75% of all recurrences will make themselves known during the first 24 months after surgery.

- The majority of patients who develop a recurrence of colon or rectal cancer cannot be cured of it.

So there you have it: twenty-four months. That's the magic number. I had thought that if I *did* happen to develop another cancer, it would be years and years down the road. At 44 years old, I figured that I might have another 40 years in me, and that if cancer came again, it would be much, much later in life, when I wouldn't mind shuffling off this mortal coil. But twenty-four months. Yipes.

I'm glad to know what I know. I do not feel that my future is blighted and that I'm sure to die of this disease. But I am rather startled. I know that Dr. C. in Victoria probably told me all these statistics, but I'm not very good at listening to numbers. I never thought I'd be one of these numbers. And one can only absorb so much at a time.

But when the rain finally came, suffice it to say that by then there wasn't much left of my mascara to run down my cheeks.

It had already been washed away.

So much depends
Upon a red wheel barrow
Glazed with rain water
Beside the white chickens

The Red Wheelbarrow, E.E. Cummings

May 10, 2008

I Surrender

At my last treatment I talked with the woman who does the healing touch, or relaxation therapy. She is a lovely, gentle woman who has helped me get through many sessions of chemo. I told her how I had begun to be able to let go of my anxiety about the treatments and sort of surrender to the experience instead of fight it. She laughed out loud, clapped her hands like an excited child and swooped down to kiss the top of my head: a sweet and loving gesture that touched me to the core. I've met so many warm, kind, strong people who have cared for me so deeply and powerfully.

She told me that she has overheard many conversations in the chemo room, and most of them revolve around people's response to their cancer, and the treatment, and how they are going to "fight this thing" or how they are going to "beat it." And as they speak, their body tightens, and their face hardens and she can see tension in every line. I've seen it too: at the lodge in Victoria, and in the chemo room at the hospital. And I do understand it, to an extent: we all want to live, and we all want to be well and healthy and to be *active* in our experiences. We *don't* want to lie down and be vanquished; we *don't* want to be helpless, powerless, voiceless. I've been there myself: mute and anguished at what was being done to me.

But Gayle raised an interesting point. She said that when we fight, every part of us is taut and hard; nothing can flow in us when we are so tight, and she really feels that this can block or hinder whatever good the medicine accomplishes in our bodies. When we give up that fight, our body relaxes, and rests, and there is the possibility of movement and flow.

I don't really know about all that, but it does seem to make sense to me. After my last treatment, I had a couple of days of pretty intense pain—intestinal cramping. At first I felt sort of angry that I was having these pains: I remembered them after my radiation, and they were so debilitating, and I hated the thought that they had returned to plague me. So I tried to ignore them. I got up from my chaise longue, and attempted to sit at the computer and work on my grad speech. I couldn't do it—the pain was too intense to allow me to sit comfortably. I squirmed around a bit, and tried to change my position. I held my breath through each wave; I tensed up; I fought it.

And then I remembered.

I got up from the desk, stretched out on the couch and gave up.

I gave up the fight and surrendered to the pain.

And found rest.

When I felt the pain begin, I breathed it out and imagined I could see it leaving through my fingertips. I focussed on keeping my body relaxed and just letting my body do what it needed to do. I kept my thoughts focussed on letting go rather than on holding in. And then I remembered that I had done something similar when I was in labour. When I could feel a contraction beginning, I stretched out my hands, breathed very hard, and imagined the pain building to a certain point, and then flowing out through my fingertips. I could almost see it. And now I imagined that I could see the pain leaving as I surrendered to it.

The power of surrendering.

Surrendering gets such bad press. In movies, surrendering is always the last-ditch attempt to preserve life and property. And it's always accompanied by white flags and shamefaced resignation. It is considered weak and cowardly. But I wonder if surrendering has more power than we imagine.

What if I surrendered to other painful things in my life rather than fighting? What might happen?

What if I surrendered to my fears about my health?

Whenever I think about the cancer returning, my body tightens, my breathing quickens, and I feel an inward trembling. And my first response is to fight it: I grit my teeth, clench my hands and mutter, "It is *not* coming back. I am *not* going to die from this." But what if I surrendered to it? To the fear and to the cancer. There is a certain amount of peace involved in giving up, or giving in; and I'm beginning to understand that it is not necessarily a weakness to give in. In some ways, I feel stronger and more courageous when I acquiesce to the inevitable. I feel more calm and more centred. I am where I am today because God brought me here, and He may take me somewhere else tomorrow, or a year from now, or two. And I can surrender to that. To be at the centre of God's will and to know it is a powerful place to be.

What if I surrendered to other things as well? My shyness? My awkwardness? My complete inability to articulate my thoughts? To speak?

What if I gave in and stopped fighting to be someone I'm not? What if I calmly accepted all those flaws and stopped trying to force myself to change? What power might result from that capitulation?

I don't know, but I'm going to think about it.

June 5, 2008

Finished

I wrote this in my journal almost three weeks ago and haven't taken the time to put it in this blog. I've been busy and tired, and tired and busy. I've begun to think I am well, and as a result have over-extended myself to the point of utter exhaustion. The road back to strength and wellness is longer than I anticipated. And fraught with such conflicting emotions. That's the real reason I haven't written–I don't really know what to feel, or how to express what's in my heart. I think I *should* feel happy, but I don't yet.

Here's what I wrote three weeks ago at Tyee Spit:

Tomorrow is the day I *would* be going for a treatment. I *would* have had my bloodwork done today, and tomorrow I would be hooked up that machine and be drifting away from myself. Even now I feel that horrible taste rising up in the back of my throat and gagging me.

But, I don't have to have blood taken today, and I don't have to have a treatment tomorrow.

I am finished.

I know I ought to be elated: jumping for joy, delighted, relieved, ecstatic. And I am, sometimes. But it also seems so unreal. So hard to fathom. So frightening.

I've read that as long as people are being treated for their cancer, they can cope with their reality. It is difficult and painful, but they feel safe knowing that something powerful is being done to bring about healing and wholeness. But afterwards, when treatments have ended, there is a sense of panic. What if it wasn't enough?

I catch myself with that clutch of panic at my heart sometimes. Teary, frightened, confused. At a loss. My entire year has been carefully plotted out for me by others, and now it's almost as if I don't know what to do. I need to remember what it's like to be well. To embrace life. To move forward.

When Geri removed my PICC line, I felt a little moment of panic. I wanted her to take it out, to set me free, but at the same time, I was frightened. And now, when I look down at my arm, I see only the faintest trace of where the catheter pierced my skin. It gives me such a sense of unreality: almost as if it never was. And I wonder if all the other scars will also fade, leaving me with only the faintest memory of this year. I don't want them to fade away completely. I don't want to forget. People have said to me so many times in the last week or so, "You're done! You can finally put all this behind you." But I don't want to leave it all behind. God has blessed me in such a powerful and profound way, and I think I'm afraid that somehow I will lose the blessing as life takes over.

After she took the PICC out, Geri seized me in a fierce embrace and said, "You've been through so much, and you did it."

I cried and clung to her, and felt a sense of triumph, or accomplishment, or something. It was strange. It's not as though I had actually *done* anything. Maybe what I was experiencing was a sense of completion: I had made it to the end and was still standing. I can take some satisfaction in that.

I am finished the chapter, but not the book.

And I think *that's* why I feel such conflicting emotions. People keep saying to me, "Oh, I'm so glad it's over. I'm so glad you're finished." I smile and agree—and I *am* glad that the chemo is over.

I do have a sense of peace. I am hopeful. I am anticipating a return to health and strength.

But it's not over.

When I left the doctor, after that last treatment, she handed me a paper entitled "Letter for Colorectal Cancer patients." It maps out years of follow-up:

- History and physical exam every three months for the first three years, then every six months for two additional years.

- Rectal exam at least yearly.

- Colonoscopy within one year following surgery (mine is already booked for September).

- Tumour markers checked at each visit.

- Liver imaging done every six months for three years, then annually for two more years.

- Chest x-rays every six months for five years.

I'm glad for the follow-up. I'm grateful that I live in an age when such things are possible. I'm relieved that doctors will be checking my organs and orifices. And I'm eager for that scope: I will have no rest until I have that colonoscopy in September.

I'm finished the chapter, but not the book.

Remembering

As a father has compassion on his children, so the Lord has compassion on those who fear him; for he knows how we are formed, he remembers that we are dust.

Sometimes I forget that I am dust. I meander through my days, not paying much attention to the thousands of little decisions I make as I live my life: decisions that either draw me closer to God, or further away from Him. And then suddenly I look at something I've done, and I see the utter depravity of my character, and I am appalled at myself. And I wonder how I got there. I've wandered along thinking that I was okay—better than okay. Close to God. Loving Him. Pleasing Him. And then it all comes tumbling down around my ears, and I see myself the way I really am: minus the pretty facades I've erected. And I wince, knowing that even now, I'm only seeing a fraction of what God sees, and knowing that if I saw it all, I would be crushed under the weight of my sin.

But I'm glad: it's good to remember that I am dust. And that God loves me and is pleased with me despite my dustiness. The irony is me thinking that it is my actions that please God, when really it is not about anything I do or don't do. God sees me through the mantle of Christ's sacrifice, through the curtain of Christ's atonement. But it is good for me to see a glimpse of myself, if only to forestall any self-congratulatory feelings I might be developing. I find it interesting that I do not feel the self-loathing I would normally feel under these circumstances; nor do I hear the refrain "Stupid, stupid, stupid" that often echoes through my mind. I can let go of that, and be resigned to my human frailties.

I remember that I am dust, and that God loves me. I am so grateful.

June 9, 2008

Joy in the Journey

I wrote a couple of days ago that I didn't think I would have any rest until my colonoscopy in September. I don't think I feel the same anymore. I think I'm willing to surrender to the "unknowing."

I read the other day that "an unanswered question is a fine traveling companion. It sharpens your eye for the road."

I like that. It means that life is about more than answers. The answers are a side benefit, but not the destination.

I've avoided using the imagery of a journey up until now—I've thought it clichéd and obvious—but I have to bow to the inevitable. Life *is* like a journey. And I've always been more a destination kind of person than a joy-in-the-journey kind. Whenever Bryan and I have taken a road trip, I've always gone into it thinking that I would be flexible, and let the road take us where it would. But the reality has never fulfilled that intention. The first day or two might be relaxed and spontaneous, but by the third day, the destination is burning in my consciousness, and I want to reach it in as short a time as possible. I become blind to the road itself and only have eyes for the end of the road.

But I suppose if I don't *know* the end of the road, I might be able to look at the scenery along the way. I might even spot the bags of gold that God drops in my path—now I might recognize them for what they are. Before this year, I might have seen them as dusty rocks that might trip me. I would have kicked them impatiently out of my way, or stepped over them with a grimace of distaste. I never would have stopped, never would have picked them up to look inside. Never would have found the blessing.

Maybe my eyes *have* been sharpened.

June 24, 2008

Returning

Not sure who has been teaching my daughter about various plagues, but she finds the subject endlessly fascinating.

Anna: Mummy, I'm glad people don't die from Black Plague or Husha Husha anymore.

Me: I'm glad too, honey.

Anna: I'm glad people don't die from ... (a wide-eyed, horrified stare fills her eyes)

Anna: Mummy, people don't die of cancer, do they? (long pause as I force my voice to respond without trembling)

Me: Yes, darling, sometimes people *do* die from cancer. (another long pause, punctuated by a couple of gulps.)

Anna: Whew ... I'm sure glad *you* didn't die, Mummy. You are very special to me.

Whew, I'm glad I didn't die, too. And I'm glad that my strength is returning and that I feel real again. I was walking along the other day, the sun was shining and I felt happy. I almost stopped dead in my tracks as this thought flitted through my head: "I feel well ... I *am* well!"

It's much better now, but a few weeks ago, I was finding the return to health and wellness quite trying. I felt a bit like an interloper, an impostor—like I was elbowing my way into a world where I had no place. It reminded me a little of returning home after Lois died and after my nana died. I remember going out in public and being sort of appalled that life for others had gone on while mine had been devastated. I heard people laughing and talking, and felt I couldn't join in—as if I had lost the gifts of laughter and sharing. I felt that I had been somewhere that others had not been, and therefore they couldn't understand my heart.

I felt like Luna Lovegood. Because she had experienced death, she could see the thestrals when no one else could.

It's not that no one but me has ever seen death or sorrow, it's just that mine was recent. Mine was about Lois ... about Nana. Mine sorrow was my own.

I think we can certainly empathize with others, but rarely can we really enter into someone else's pain.

And that's a little how I have felt these last weeks as I have entered back into life. I have walked through the valley of the shadow of death, and now I am back among the living.

It is very strange.

And yet, each week has become easier and more natural and I sometimes forget that I have been sick. Sometimes.

I went out with friends last night, and had a *great* time. We laughed and told stories and laughed more.

But when I got home, I reviewed the conversations we had, and I was sort of horrified by how many times I had talked about my illness. I haven't done that for weeks. For weeks, I have worked, I've gone on field trips with my kids, taken them to swim practice, visited my parents, had dinner with friends, and lived without endlessly talking about my health.

But last night I did.

Yesterday morning someone told me about the death of an acquaintance. She had died from cancer.

Years ago she had struggled through breast cancer and had recovered.

But last year the cancer had spread throughout her body. And then she died.

When I heard the news, I tried to think of her family and friends, but when it came down to it, I could only think of myself. The tears rose in my eyes, and I had to leave the room.

And cry by myself in the bathroom.

I know that people die from cancer. But it still gives me the wiggins.

I felt badly for my friend who had told the news. She had to tell me: I needed to know. It's more important to know than to be "protected" from "bad" news. I don't want to be "protected," I want to be a participant in life. But that can be painful and hard, and I know my friend felt badly.

And I think that's why I talked about it last night.

I mostly talked about the funny stuff: the stuff that made me laugh.

But lurking around in the back of my mind was the knowledge that people die from cancer.

July 16, 2008

Putting My Behind in the Past

I was at a hafla a couple of weeks ago—a party with music, food and belly-dancing. It was held in the beautiful backyard of my dance teacher. I had a hard time deciding if I would attend the party: I hadn't danced all year, and felt very reticent about the dance, the people, the visiting. Parties are always hard for me because I'm so awkward in social situations—and an event with dancing makes me feel even more awkward. And then there was the matter of what to wear: I don't really have an outfit, and most of the other women have lots of glittery, beautiful, sparkly outfits. And then there was my physical exhaustion.

I've been doing too much, and really paying for it. June is a busy month anyway—sports day, field trips, clubs, dance recitals, piano recitals, graduation, and work. I worked in June. Probably not a smart move, but at the time, I thought I could do it. And I did. But I was more tired than I thought I would be. And I was discouraged by that. I think I jumped back into life, right into the deep end, and I've been frantically treading water trying to keep my head above the water line.

So when it came to the hafla, I just didn't know what to do.

And then I remembered how kind and supportive my dance friends had been: the gifts and cards, the notes and messages. And I remembered how much I love to dance—how much I love the music—how much I love my Shannon and how I love to watch her dance, and I decided to go, but I thought I would just wear street clothes.

But as I was getting ready, I looked at my dance things, and I remembered that I did have a crop top, and some sparkly things. But I have a really big scar on my belly, and I feel self-conscious about it.

I stood in my room for a few minutes, holding the top and wondering. And then a thought flashed across my consciousness: "I almost died this year. I can wear any freakin' thing I want to wear!"

Later, at the party, when people were saying how glad they were that I came, I told them about my struggle earlier in the evening, and when I came to that point, and shouted, "I almost died this year ..." there was a sudden hush.

I said, "I guess I probably should stop saying that. It makes people feel uncomfortable."

Everyone hastened to say that it didn't make them uncomfortable at all, but they were lying. I could tell by the looks on their faces.

My teacher said, "No, I think it's good that you say it. It's true, and you need to say it ... But maybe you should change it around and say, 'I didn't die this year.'"

Brilliant.

I *didn't* die this year. Now *that's* something to dance about.

After I spoke at grad, one of the moms came and thanked me. She said that now that her last child had graduated, she and her husband were going to take some time to relax and have fun. She said, "You know, sometimes you just have to take time to dance." And she glanced at me meaningfully. "I hope you're going to take some time to dance this summer."

Yes.

I said to my dancing friends that I felt that I needed to do something to mark this year. Something to celebrate the year and bring some sort of closure, or something. I don't really know how to express it. One of my friends from the cancer clinic is a kayaker with lots of experience navigating rivers. She pictures her experience with cancer as a journey in which she has had to navigate through the "rapids" of radiation and the pain of recovery towards the quiet waters of wellness. She is making a quilt that represents this journey. It's a beautiful thought, and I'm sure the making of the quilt is therapeutic and healing.

Quilting is not my thing. I'm not really sure what my thing is. But I have been thinking about how I would like to mark the year. And when I said so to my dancing friends, one said, "You could get your eyebrow pierced."

No. That's not it.

Another squealed, "Oooh! You could get a tattoo!"

No. That's not it either.

In view of these suggestions, I didn't want to admit that I just wanted to buy a pair of shoes.

Not really.

It could be that this blog is the thing that brings meaning to my year.

It's been my way of dealing with the whole experience all along. Maybe it's enough to think about it, write about it, share it in some small way.

I don't know.

My roommate from Victoria gave me a scrapbook and encouraged me to scrapbook the experience. She has photos and things from her time at the clinic, and she is going to scrapbook.

I'm not so good at keeping things. But maybe I'll scrapbook.

I don't really know where I'm going with this post. I have a lot of thoughts swirling through my mind, and I'm having a hard time sorting through them all. I went for my follow-up in Victoria last week, and I think it upset me more than I realized at the time. I keep fooling myself into thinking that it's over, and it's not. It's okay that it's not over, and I'm used to having these thoughts hovering on the edges of my mind. I'm resigned to it in a way; but when they are forced to the forefront again, it's jarring, and it takes me a few days to find equanimity again. Little vague ribbons of sadness and loss drift around me, hindering me.

As I read what I've written, I realize that it sounds as though I think I need to be moving ahead in some way. But I think I have it all wrong. Who says I have to make any progress at all? Who says I have to be moving ahead? Forward? Who says I have to put anything *behind* me at all?

Hmmm. I'll have to think about this.

July 17, 2008

Que Sera, Sera

When I read what I wrote earlier, I had a sudden realization.

I think what I've been trying to do with all this activity is to put my illness behind me. Pretend it never happened. Be the person I was a year ago. Return to myself.

But the truth is that I'll never be that person again.

And strangely, for today at least, this thought brings no sadness, just a sense of arriving, finally, at a truth that brings strength and peace—almost a sense of fulfillment. I can't really explain it today. Yesterday I felt almost grief-stricken, but the night brought perspective, peace and purpose (oooh, I could preach a three-point sermon on that!).

I read this recently:

"Until we stop ourselves, or more often, have been stopped, we hope to put certain of life's events 'behind us' and get on with our living. After we stop we see that certain of life's issues will be with us as long as we live. We will pass through them again and again, each time with a new story, each time with a greater understanding, until they become indistinguishable from our blessing and our wisdom" (Rachel Naomi Remen).

Cancer will be with me as long as I live. However long that happens to be. Last week I went for my follow-up in Victoria. There were no surprises ... Not really. I knew I would have to have CT scans every six months for the first three years. The doctor said that the tumour is unlikely to grow back in the same spot, thanks to the radiation; however, people who have had one rectal tumour are likely to grow another one. Nice. She also said that the lungs and liver are of particular concern, hence the CT scans. Nothing to raise my hackles yet. But then she said, "If we find cancer in one location, we'll just hack it out; but if we find it in more than one location there's nothing we can do about that." Now, she *may* have said "cut it out," but I heard "hack it out," I know I did. And the "nothing we can do about that" got my goat a little as well.

A couple of days ago, Anna said, "Mummy, if you died, and all of your friends died on the same day, I'd give you a really good funeral." So, I've got that to look forward to anyway.

But today, with the sun shining, I feel no sadness, no regret. Whatever will be, will be. As much as I abhor resorting to what sounds like a cliché, God in fact *does* have a plan for my life. He knows better than I do what my future holds; what is best for my children; how He will work out His purpose for all of us. I tend to get pretty self-centred and think that my life is only about me. It's not. It's about God and His greater purpose. And in some strange way, I look forward to seeing that purpose unfold.

So, I can see how this particular "life issue" of mine—this one of many "life issues"—has already brought a small morsel of wisdom, however flawed my understanding might be.

September 1, 2008

Same Time, Last Year

A year ago today, on August 31, 2007, I had the colonoscopy that revealed my cancer. So much of the day is foggy in my memory, and yet strange little details are vivid and fresh. I remember that they were running late that day, in the endoscopy suite, and there was a lot of waiting involved. In reality, the waiting was probably minor, but in my state of mind, it loomed up as vast wastelands of sluggishly ticking second hands on the clock.

I remember that one of the nurses was Paige; the other, Alexis.

I remember lying on the bed, listening to my iPod. The iPod was new, and I had just loaded it with music; I didn't know then how it would comfort me in the darkness of so many lonely nights in the hospital and in the cancer clinic.

During that wait, I remember hearing Dr. B. talk to patient after patient, all of whom had already had the procedure done. Each time the exchange went something like this:

"Well, Mr. X., everything looks clear. No polyps. Nothing to worry about. No cancer at all."

"Thank you, Doctor."

or

"Well, Mrs. B.—we found a few polyps, but we nipped them out. They don't look cancerous, so you'll be just fine,"

"Thank you, Doctor."

or

"Well. Mr. T.—you're amazing, you are! Everything is fine. Nothing to worry about at all. You just keep going and going. Good for you."

"Thank you, Doctor."

After listening to several of these conversations, I remember thinking to myself, "There are at least ten people here. We can't *all* be well; the odds are against us. One of us *must* have cancer. It's going to be me, I just know it."

And as Paige came to wheel me into the room, I said, "I'm a little scared."

"What are you scared of?" she asked.

I was scared that I had cancer, of course; but I couldn't say the word. It was almost as if I thought that I could speak it into being. That if I said it out loud, it would be true.

"I'm just scared," I said.

I remember that Dr. C. said, "Oops," as he put the needle in my arm, and I said, "Now *that* is a word that should not be heard in an operating room."

He grinned.

I was serious.

Dr. B. came in. He put on some music, and I faded out.

I came to as they were wheeling me out of the room. I was not fully conscious, but I heard people talking about a CT scan. I somehow knew they were talking about me.

I began to cry.

Dr. B. came over.

"Why are you crying?" he said.

"I'm scared."

"Why are you scared?" he asked.

I was afraid that I had cancer, of course; but again, I couldn't say the word, so again I just said, "I'm scared."

He touched my shoulder and said, "Oh, Lovey. You're going to be fine."

I knew that he couldn't *know* that I would be fine, but I liked him saying it. I liked him using the word "Lovey"—it's the name I have called my children since they were babies, and his use of the word was inexpressibly comforting to me.

I faded out again.

"Oh good," I heard a nurse say. "Here is her husband."

Dr. B. motioned him over, and they spoke; but their words were indistinct to me.

Bryan opened the curtain. I looked at him; his eyes were full of tears. He stumbled towards me and collapsed into my arms.

"Oh good," said Paige. "Your husband is here."

"Yes," I said. "And as you can see, he is being a great help to me."

She laughed.

Later Dr. B. came to my bedside. He sat down and looked at his hands.

"This is the part of my job that I really hate."

I thought to myself, "You cannot hate saying it nearly as much as I hate hearing it."

He told us more.

I remember tearing up again, and apologizing: "It's just that I have two little kids at home, and they are really young," I cried.

I saw the nurses across the room look at each other and start whispering.

Dr. B. called one of the nurses over, and asked her to tell me about her mother, who had just finished all her treatments for the same kind of cancer.

"She's doing really well now, isn't she?" he prompted.

The nurse nodded vigorously and assured me that her mother was feeling great, but that I needed to know that it took a full year for her to really get through it all.

"A year?" I thought. "I can't do it."

I remember that as I was leaving the room to go have my CT scan, Dr. B. half turned towards me and said, "My fiancée is doing your scan." And he smiled a sweet, proud, delighted kind of smile, and I said, "Awww, really?" It seemed so sweet and cute and human for him to tell me that.

And she was so kind and understanding and calming as she explained the procedure and did the scan.

I remember going back to my room and finding a flower on my bed. Paige had left it for me.

I saw her later, in the hall, and she hugged me tight and wished me well.

I remember feeling dazed and exhausted as we left the building, and knowing that it was only going to get worse as we went to tell all the people who love us that I was very sick. I didn't want to do it. I didn't know how I could do it. And I don't think I was able to say the word "cancer." I still couldn't say it.

I remember all my friends: what they did and what they said. I remember that it broke my heart.

And I knew that it was just the beginning.

2010

February 26, 2010

Not Today

Even though in the deepest part of my heart I knew that this wasn't over, I always hoped beyond hope that it was.

But it's not.

The cancer is back.

Sometimes I say, "My cancer is back."

But today I want no part of it.

Today, just now, I am overwhelmed by that knowledge.

I have a pain in my back. It is probably a slightly pulled muscle from lifting a very heavy briefcase full of unfinished marking. But I know it's cancer.

Because every unexplained ache, or upset tummy, or shortness of breath, or fatigue is cancer to me now.

I hate it.

Most of the time, I can be pretty brave about it, and continue doing my life, but I know I'm going to have moments like this, when it all comes crashing down on me.

Because yesterday I went to the funeral of a friend.

She died of cancer.

She was diagnosed after I was; she was treated and restored to health for a time.

And now she is dead.

Her white casket stood at the front of the church.

Her husband and her children (adults now, but I taught them when they were young) were there too. Sometimes weeping, sometimes smiling, sometimes just gazing ahead, eyes glazed with grief.

My husband sat beside me, surreptitiously wiping his eyes.

My friend sat on the other side, sobs howling inside, raging to get out.

I sat stunned and heavy.

Her son gave a glorious eulogy. He spoke of how cancer had not defeated them. Instead, it had reconciled them as a family, renewed their faith, reaffirmed their love for one another, blessed them in the knowledge of how much their friends love them, and filled them with a deeper understanding of God's mercies.

Sometimes I think that I don't want any of that.

I know it's true, but not today.

Today, I just want to be well.

I want to run.

I want to see my son graduate and help my daughter choose her wedding dress.

I want to grow old with my husband.

> *Say to those with fearful hearts,*
> *'Be strong, do not fear;*
> *your God will come.*
> *he will come with vengeance,*
> *with divine retribution*
> *he will come to save you.'*

Isaiah 35:4

Doing the Hokey Pokey

I saw a bumper sticker the other day. It said: "What if doing the Hokey Pokey *is* what it's all about?"

I laughed, and thought of Paula, and the time she made me stand up at the front at a playschool tea and do the Hokey Pokey in front of all the parents and grandparents.

Good times.

You know, people don't realize that I am a very shy person.

They're always asking me to stand up in front of people and do things.

Doing the Hokey Pokey.

The more I thought about it, the more I came to think that there is a grain of truth in that statement.

What do you do in the Hokey Pokey?

> *You put your right hand in,*
> *you take your right hand out,*
> *You put your right hand in*
> *And you shake it all about.*
> *You do the hokey pokey, and you turn yourself around,*
> *That's what it's all about.*

But that's *not* what it's *all* about, because then you have to do it all over again with your left hand.

And then you think, "Okay, I get it ... *that's* what it's *all* about."

But you're *not* done.

You have to put your right foot in, and then your left foot in, and then your head.

And you think you're finally done.

But you're not, because then you have to put your whole body in.

It's very exhausting.

Which is why teachers of small children like it.

I wonder if I could get junior high kids to do the Hokey Pokey.

I think one of the reasons why the Hokey Pokey is so exhausting is because you keep thinking that it's over ... That you've done all the verses, and that you're finally finished. But you're never finished.

Life *is* a little bit like doing the Hokey Pokey.

Have you ever been through something difficult? A time when you had to rely on God for something—strength, patience, safety, health? A time when you knew that it was just you and God? And you knew that if you didn't cling to Him, you would just slide into the abyss?

If you're alive, and if you have a relationship with God, then I'm sure you've had times like this. It might have been just a moment, or it may have lingered for months, or even years.

And sometimes, when it is all over, we can look back and see how God touched our life in the midst of that darkness. We see a truth we learned, or a little growth spurt we experienced, or a deepening of our relationship with God.

And we might be tempted to think that we figured it all out. That we know the *whys*.

I can't tell you how many times I have figured out what life is all about. Or at least, what my life is all about.

And I'd say to God, "*Oh!* I get it! *That's* what this is all about!" And I'd refer to the lesson I thought I had learned through it all.

Have you ever read *The Bike Lesson* by Stan and Jan Berenstein?

I'd be like those little bears: "Thank you, thank you, now I see. That was a very good lesson for me."

But like the Hokey Pokey, I'd turn myself about and find myself learning the same lesson again later on. The circumstances might be different, but the "lesson" was similar.

It's like there's an overarching theme to my life.

It's different for all of us, but for me, this overarching theme has often had to do with learning how to let go of my expectations about what my life is going to be like.

Learning how to relinquish this obsessive need to control everything, and to make everything go *my* way.

So, thinking in terms of this overarching theme, I've begun to think of my life as a book. Divided into episodes, or short stories, linked by a common theme—or a number of common themes. And these stories are building to some sort of climax.

I've always thought in stories. At night, before I went to sleep, I would make up stories in my head. Of course, I was always the main character, and I was always heroic and adventurous and talented and beautiful.

Did I mention that the stories were always about me?

And I was always heroic.

So, realizing that my life is like a book, sort of a collection of short stories that build on a theme, is not really a new thing.

What *is* new, is that I've just had a startling epiphany.

I really did have this epiphany.

It happened last week.

I am *not* the main character of my stories. In fact, my life story isn't really about *me* at all. *And* I'm not going to really know what it was all about until it's over and I get to sit down and have a cup of coffee with the author.

There have been lots of times when I thought I knew what it was about, or at least what the recurring themes were, but now I'm not so sure. Its plot is much more intricate and its themes more far-reaching that I can possibly imagine.

"Many are the plans in a man's heart, but it is the *Lord's* purpose that prevails."

I was not the One who picked up a pen and began the story, and I won't be the One who writes "The End" on the last page.

God is the author of my life story.

and

He is the main character.

And so, as a mere supporting character, it's not really up to me what belongs in the story. I don't get to say to the author, "You know that plot twist you're planning on page 27? Yeah, that's not going to work. I don't want to be married for eleven years before I finally get to have a baby. Because then I'll be *old*, and the whole Abraham and Sarah thing has already been done."

or

"I don't think that cancer plotline is the way to go. I mean, haven't we all read enough stories about mothers dying of cancer? It just sounds so cliché, so cheesy. Let's not go there. You're going to have to do a major rewrite."

Many are the plans in a man's heart, but it is the *Lord's* purpose that prevails.

I read a book last summer that gave me some new insights about the Fall.

So, there's this tree in the Garden of Eden. The Tree of the Knowledge of Good and Evil.

A tree of knowledge, or understanding, or comprehension, or expertise.

And God says to Adam, "You are free to eat from any tree in the garden; but you must not eat from the Tree of the Knowledge of Good and Evil, for when you eat of it you will surely die."

I noticed a couple of things when I read this the other night: first, Eve wasn't there. She hadn't even been created yet. Second: God did not say "for *if* you eat of it you will surely die." He said, "for *when* you eat of it you will surely die."

He already knew the plotline. He wasn't making it up as he went.

So, Eve was created, and the man and his wife were naked, and were content with that.

And soon, along came the serpent that convinced Eve that God had a hidden agenda in his decree about the fruit. The serpent convinced Eve that God did not want them to know that the fruit would open their eyes, and that they would be like God, knowing good and evil. That is, *understanding* good and evil; *comprehending* good and evil; having an *expertise* about good and evil.

And so, Adam and Eve, desirous of gaining that "wisdom" or "expertise," ate the fruit. As soon as their lips touched that fruit, in that instant of their disobedience, something momentous happened.

They had a fallen nature.

They could never "be like God," as the serpent had said.

And they could never have a knowledge of good and evil. Not a true knowledge. Their understanding, their comprehension, their expertise was filtered through their fallen nature.

Because what did they do first? They looked at themselves and at each other and said, "Wow. We're naked. Naked is bad. We need to cover up."

Now, who told them that naked is bad, or that seeing your

husband or wife naked is bad? No one. They made a judgement based on their so-called expertise, filtered through their fallen nature.

And humankind has been doing the same for thousands of years. We think we know what is good and what is evil.

We have a propensity to make judgements about the things that come into our lives, to declare whether something is good or bad in our life.

Going back to my story illustration, we make judgements about what happens in our story based on whether things make us happy or sad. If it makes us happy, it must be a good thing. If it makes us sad, or causes pain, it must be a bad thing.

And we think we can figure out what it all means. We do the hokey pokey and we turn ourselves around—and we decide "*That's* what it's all about."

Two years ago, I had rectal cancer. I had surgery, and months of radiation and chemo.

And God was there in power, refining me through fire.

And I was better.

And I went back to work.

And I was so happy.

But about two months ago, I received confirmation that the cancer had returned. And this time, it is not curable.

When I started telling people that the cancer had returned, there were a lot of different responses. But one response that I found a bit puzzling was when people said to me, "Cancer is *never* part of God's plan!"

Really?

Well, it certainly wasn't my plan.

But I'm not the one writing the book.

Hebrews 12:2 says, "Let us fix our eyes on Jesus, the author and perfecter of our faith, who for the joy set before him endured the cross, scorning its shame, and sat down at the right hand of God."

He is the *author* and *perfecter* of my *faith*.

* Notice that it says *faith* not *life*—this tells me that my faith is more valuable to God than my life is.

So, maybe God will write some really hard things into my life to perfect my faith, or to "finish" my faith, as the King James version says.

So, I don't want to say that cancer is a bad thing in my life, that it's evil. I don't want to say that if God's big plan is to use cancer to perfect my faith.

And not just my faith.

My little baby girl is seven years old; her brother is ten. My plan is to be a mother to my children, and to raise them as best as I can: to help my daughter choose a wedding gown; to watch my son deliver the valedictory address at his graduation. My plan is to grow old with my husband.

Many are the plans in a man's heart, but it is the *Lord's* purpose that prevails.

But God is writing a really big story, and I am not the main character. *He* is the main character of my story. And He has already designed my story to perfect my faith.

It's not just my faith that's being finished here. The little collection of short stories that makes up my life is connected to the stories that make up Laurie's life, and her collection is connected to Lynay's, and Lynay's is connected to Tammie's, and so on.

The story God is writing is *huge*.

A couple of weeks ago, my surgeon said to me, "You must feel as though you've landed in the deep water without a life preserver. I wish I could throw you a life preserver, but I don't know which one to throw."

They can't get to the bottom of this cancer. It's a tricky one, and they don't know how to treat it yet.

So I went home and thought about what he had said; and a few days later I wrote him a note. I said: I already have a life preserver. His name is Jesus, and no matter how deep the water gets, or how rough the waves, I know that He will encircle me with His arms and keep me safe. He holds my life and keeps me from sinking.

I told him that my children are praying for God to dissolve the cancer and make me whole. I let them pray like that, and I told him that whether God heals me or not, my life is in His hands and I trust Him.

My surgeon's faith is part of the story, too. And God's plans will prevail.

Just after my son was born, the labour and delivery nurse turned around and said, "Is everyone in this room a Christian?" She had heard us praying during the labour.

We all laughed and said, "Yes!"

She picked up my little baby boy and prayed a beautiful prayer of anointing. She prayed that the Lord would raise him up to be a prophet of God.

Today I know that the beautiful faith of this little ten-year-old boy is being refined by the fire. I've heard him pray, "Oh Lord, it says in the Psalms that you will cover us with your feathers, and under your wings we will find refuge. Oh, Lord, we need those wings and feathers now."

And I think to myself, well, Nathan is part of this big huge plan of God, too. Maybe this is part of how God plans to equip him

---

for his life's work.

Nathan's faith is part of the story.

When I first heard the new diagnosis a few weeks ago, I was lost in despair for a few weeks. This is not a curable situation. I can be treated for a time, but I cannot be cured. Not by medicine, anyway.

So, that was a little hard to take.

I just didn't understand.

I didn't understand why God would allow me to have two little babies, only to take me away from them before they are grown.

I didn't understand how He would let me do the job I love, only to make me give it up.

I wasn't angry at God; I just didn't get it.

So I said to Him, "I just don't get it. I need you to help me."

He said, "Trust me."

He said, "You need to turn from your despair. I don't want 'incurable' to be your word. I am giving you a new word: *hope*."

And as soon as He impressed that word upon me, I felt it flutter to life in my heart.

I know a lot of people have been praying for that to happen; for me to release my fear and despair to God and be filled with *hope*.

And it happened.

The very next day I went to school. It was chapel day, and I walked in a bit late. I almost didn't go. I almost stayed behind to get caught up on some things. But I felt a little tug, and I went.

I walked in just in time to hear Stephanie Wilkenson say, "We need to humble ourselves right where we are and get on our knees and pray that she will be healed." And she said that anyone who wanted to could come to the front and pray.

I thought, "Uh oh, I think she's talking about me." So I went over to my friend Sarah, who's in grade twelve, and said, "Is she talking about me?"

She nodded.

We threw our arms around each other and stood there crying.

And I thought of how thankful I am for this young woman. I first met her when she was a baby, and now she is holding me close and sustaining me. My story is part of her story, too.

Up until the day before, whenever anyone said that they were praying that God would heal me, I would say, "You go ahead and pray that. I can't pray that yet."

It wasn't in my heart. I had no hope.

But God had given me a new word.

"Against all hope, Abraham in hope believed and so became the father of many nations."

Even when it didn't make any sense, God helped Abraham to act in hope."

And so in hope, I grabbed Sarah's hand and we went to the front of chapel. We knelt down and began to cry and pray, just silently at first. Within seconds, I could feel kids crowding around me, kneeling down, reaching out to touch me, praying out in loud voices asking God to heal me. Soon most of the chapel band had stopped playing, and were clustered around me, praying. It was powerful, and God was moving.

It went on for awhile, and then we returned to our seats.

What I didn't know, but found out by talking to some of the other kids later in class, was that kids all over the room just dropped to their knees right where they were, to pray. Kids that

I would never have expected to be so bold were praying right there, on their knees.

And I was completely overwhelmed.

First, because I felt so loved and cared for.

But more importantly, because I saw a glimpse into that big huge plan of God's.

He is not just perfecting my faith. He is perfecting the faith of all those kids at the Christian school.

And together we are learning that His hope "is an anchor for the soul, firm and secure ..." as Hebrews 6:19 says.

I told the kids that I was searching out *hope* verses in the Bible; and every day or so, I bring a new one and put it on my white board.

And you know what?

Now kids are bringing me hope verses, and writing them on the white board.

So, I don't want to make judgements about what is good and what is bad in my life anymore.

How can cancer be bad, if that's what God brings about?

It can be painful and sorrowful and hard.

But it's not bad.

So, I guess what I'm saying is that I'm not going to do the Hokey Pokey anymore.

I'm not going to turn myself about and decide what life is all about.

I'm just going to say that it's all a lot bigger and more complicated than I thought.

And I'm just going to leave that with God.

He knows the plotline and the themes.

He knows whose stories belong together, and He is going to make sure that they touch.

I just need to trust Him.

> *He is the Rock, his works are perfect, and all his ways are just.*
> *A faithful God who does no wrong, upright and just is he.*

April 29, 2010

The Healing Rooms

I went to the Healing Rooms today. This is a place where people come together to pray for anyone who comes, anyone who wants to be healed, or who wants to meet with God.

I had never been to the Healing Rooms before. I always maintained that God could heal me anywhere—not solely at rooms labeled *The Healing Rooms*.

But I misunderstood.

No one at the Healing Rooms limits God.

No one thinks that healing only happens there and nowhere else.

No one thinks the rooms are anything more than just a venue, a meeting place.

I went a couple of weeks ago, and God did a powerful work in me. He showed some burdens that I was carrying, burdens that I needed to release to Him. While the people were praying (just two people, not a throng), I envisioned God reaching into my heart and pulling out a thick, black stump with long, gangly roots encrusted with dirt. I knew it was the burden I had been carrying for thirty years: the burning sense that it was *my* responsibility to bring my dad to a saving faith in Jesus.

I let that burden go, and since then God has shown me others that I also needed to release to Him.

So, I decided to go again. I took Laurie with me.

I somehow knew she needed to be there too. She is a part of me, and what is happening in me right now is happening in her.

Today they wanted me to come in alone. Mostly because they

pray in advance of prayer with the client, and they need to feel a sense of agreement in prayer, and when they don't know the people involved, this can be difficult.

But I knew that Laurie had to come in, too. So I did what I very rarely do; I insisted. They thought it was because I was afraid to come in by myself, but I knew that God wanted us to be together.

This story could go on forever, so I'll try to condense.

They talked about taking things slowly, and spending time listening and waiting for God. They spoke of the complexities of healing, and how it is so much more than the physical body. They spoke of bringing hope, and speaking words of peace into the trauma.

Then they began to pray.

At first the man said, "Sandy, I'm sensing that today has so much to do with your heart. Does this resonate with you?" So, I told them about what had happened last time, and how God had already been working in my heart.

Then he prayed for a bit, and he said, "Sandy, I sense that you have always been a giving person ... that you love to give ... but you have had a very difficult time receiving ... In fact, you hate to receive. I sense that your giving has come out of a place of control. It makes you feel safe ... in control. Receiving makes you feel vulnerable. Even receiving from God."

And then I felt something break inside me.

I took in a great, deep, shuddering breath, and I cried out in a loud voice, "I repent! I repent, Lord! It's true!"

It was kind of funny because the whole situation is not a situation that I would ever place myself in—never! I would *never* be alone in a room with strangers yelling out my repentance. When I came to the Lord 30 years ago, I was alone, in my room, just me and God. And that's the only way I have ever really met with God.

But not today.

I kept shouting, "It's true, Lord, I repent. I repent."

And it *was* true; I had given out of a deep sense of control. And love. Love was always there, but I see now that control was there, too. Maybe a need to measure out my response; to prove my love for people and for God; to be worthy, or to make me feel as though I deserved my salvation; to work out my salvation, maybe. I don't really know yet what it was all about. I think it will take days for me to see what really happened today, but that's how it started.

And the woman said, "Okay now, Sandy, it's gone. You repented, and it's gone. Part of the past, remembered no more. Let it go."

So we did that for awhile.

And then she asked me how I was feeling.

I said, touching my upper tummy, "I feel a huge heaviness. And crowding. It's hard to breathe."

So she prayed for God to touch my body; for the cancer cell to disappear; for healing; for restoration.

And that went on for awhile.

And then the man turned to Laurie, and he said, "And, Lord, I pray for this dear woman too, that you would meet her needs."

And I said, "Yes, Lord, thank you."

And Laurie grasped my arm and said, "Sandy, have you let go of me, too?"

And I felt something break inside me, and I took a deep, shuddering breath, and I shouted, "Yes!! Yes! Yes, Lord, I release Laurie, and all the responsibility I feel for her!"

And the woman said, "Has this been an issue for long?"

Yes. I have not been able to bear the pain that I have been inflicting on her because of this illness. The pain of losing another friend to cancer. The pain of having to do this long, hard walk again, and to come out on the other side alone.

But today I let her go.

Thank you, Jesus.

The woman said, "And how do you feel now?

"I feel light."

"I feel that I am made of light."

"I am new."

Today I surrendered all.

And I laughed.

I laughed, and laughed, and laughed.

I was drunk in the spirit.

I went outside, and I looked at Laurie, and I said, "I've never been here before."

She said, "What?"

I said, "I've never been here before. With God. I am completely *free*. I am free, and new, and whole."

On the drive home I said, "You know, they told me to come back anytime I wanted."

"Good," Laurie replied.

But I always used to think that it was rather insulting to keep asking God for the same thing over and over again. It implies that He has a hearing problem, or that He forgets and needs to be reminded, or that He can't be trusted to act.

The one story that I have always hated is the story of the persistent widow. If I were God, I would hate that persistent widow; she was so annoying. When my children ask me the same thing over and over again, it just grates on my nerves and makes me want to do the opposite of what they are requesting.

Maybe that story isn't really about what God needs, but about what we need. God doesn't need to be reminded of our needs. In fact, He doesn't need to be asked at all; He knows what we need before we know it.

We need to say our needs over and over again because it helps us to remember that we are utterly reliant on God. Without Him we are nothing. Without Him we have nothing. Without Him we are lost, and naked, and alone.

When I was a child, going off to visit a friend, the last words my dad always said to me were, "Don't outstay your welcome."

So, as a child, I learned that if you stay too long at your friend's house, you won't be welcome there anymore.

If you are troublesome while you are at your friend's house, you won't be welcome.

If you ask for anything while you are at your friend's house, you won't be welcome.

Many of my friends have probably noticed that my visits to their homes have always been rather brief. To this day, I am afraid of outstaying my welcome.

And I think I have been afraid of outstaying my welcome with God.

Of asking too much.

Of asking too often.

But not today.

Today I surrendered all.

All.

And I am going to keep on asking for healing.

This morning I read about Elijah under the juniper tree asking for rain.

He bowed himself to the ground, and hid himself in his mantle, and kept on asking for rain.

He sent his servant to look over and over again; and each time his servant came back and told him that he could not see rain.

And Elijah kept on asking.

And finally, the servant said that far off in the distance, he could see a tiny little rain cloud.

It rained.

May 18, 2010

Empty Hands

Am I dying? I don't know. On Saturday, I thought I was probably going to end up in the hospital, and I wondered if I would die. And I panicked, a little bit. It wasn't that I might die, but that I hadn't finished something. I had spent hours and hours organizing my house, and buying things I thought my family would need, and sorting through trash, and endlessly *doing* things, but I hadn't spent any time writing anything down for my children, or my husband, or my friends. I had things to say, and I hadn't said them.

How do you know when you're dying? How do you know it's time? Do you wait until you *do* know, or do you just start saying things and hope that you get to repeat yourself?

Because I still have hope that I'm going to stick around for a little while longer. I believe that God is at work in my body, touching me, healing me, restoring me.

But maybe not. Maybe the healing I see in my future is the complete healing package. The ultimate healing. The moment that God flings open His kingdom to me and says, "Behold, the famine is ended. All you see before you is yours."

And so, maybe I need to start saying some things.

Someone asked me to describe what it is like to begin to come to terms with my finite-ness.

I don't know. I don't know if I can come to terms with it yet.

But I'm thinking about it.

I'm praying about it, and I'm asking God to show me.

Show me the inheritance he has for me, which is still a mystery.

Last night, while I rested, sleepless in bed, I thought of my mother-in-law. My beloved Lois. I remembered the first time I met her. It was Christmas, and Bryan had picked me up at the airport in Saskatoon and taken me to her home. She was in the living room; we walked in the back door, and I heard this really deep, smokey voice say, "Weeeeeelllllll, Darlin'."

And there she was, holding out her little gnarled hands, face wreathed in a welcoming smile.

I think going to Heaven might be like that.

I keep picturing it as a journey, but like no journey I've ever undertaken.

I *always* overplan my holidays. I overpack for my holidays. I overbuy, overdo, overthink.

But there is really no planning for this journey. No packing. In fact, I said to someone the other day that I feel the need to unpack for this journey.

We accumulate so much stuff in this life. So much flotsam and jetsam. So many superfluous items, and ideas, and opinions, and feelings. So many resentments and pettinesses. So much stuff. And for so long we think it's important. We cling to it. We grasp it.

But what do we have at the end of our lives? What can we bring to Jesus that He needs, or wants? What can we take with us into eternity?

Nothing. Just our empty hands held out in supplication to the one Who fills us and redeems us.

That's what it's like to face my finite-ness. To realize that after 47 years on this earth, I still have nothing to give Him except my heart.

And to know that my heart is all He has ever really wanted.

June 1, 2010

An Invitation to the Thirsty

I went to the Healing Rooms again last week.

Again, God met me in a way I had never met Him before. I knew I had to go there, that God hadn't finished with me yet, but I didn't really know what to expect.

As always, the prayer partners met me with words that I knew came from God; they always pray before they come out to greet you, and then they pray with you. Every time I have met with them, they have always had a word for me, or a picture for me that confirms that they have spoken to God, and that God has spoken truth to them.

This time the woman said to me, "When I was praying, I got a picture. It was a hurricane or tornado ... You know how there is a still, quiet place at the centre? That's where you are, and the wind is raging all around you, but God has you there, at the centre."

I started to cry, because for weeks, whenever I pray, I get a picture that I am in a glass cylinder that's standing in the palm of God's hand and the wind is howling around me, but I am safe. And I keep calling out to my friends who are fighting in the wind to come in where it is safe and peaceful. "Come in here!" I yell. "God is here. Right here! There's nothing to be afraid of here."

Moments like that confirm to me that God is working.

And then we prayed together. We prayed for the healing and restoration of my liver; we prayed for the cancer to leave my body; we prayed for God to fill me and my family to overflowing.

And then came something I was sort of expecting, but not really.

I knew that God wanted me there that day and that He had something for me that day. The last time I had been to the healing rooms, I knew that He had met me in a deep and profound way, but I hadn't quite let down all my defences. I had opened up to Him on a deeper level than ever before, but I had still held back that tiny bit.

Why? Why do we hold out on God? Why are we so afraid to let Him in completely? What are we afraid of? Or let me just speak for myself, because maybe I'm alone in this. What am I afraid of?

Before I came to faith in Jesus Christ, I had a friend who often invited me to church activities, and I always declined. I was afraid then that God would *get* me. I don't even know what I meant by that, but those were always the words that came to mind: "God will get me." I don't know if I thought He would change me, or get inside me, or make me do things I didn't want to do, or what. But I always knew that if I went to church, God would *get* me.

I was both attracted to and horrified by the idea. In one sense, I *wanted* God to get me. I had always believed that He existed, and I craved more; but on the other hand, He was so mysterious that I dreaded being *got* by Him. What if He didn't like what He saw? What if He destroyed me, like He did the people in Noah's day? (I was secretly haunted by the illustrations I had seen in a children's Bible at my dentist's office—pictures of terrified, drowning people begging for mercy while Noah and his family floated away in the ark. What if this mean, silvery-bearded God had no mercy for me?)

Eventually, God *did* get me. And He *did* change me, and get inside me, and ask me to do things that made me uncomfortable. But it wasn't what I had imagined. It wasn't horrifying.

But I think I always held out on Him a bit. I think that old fear made me hold out on Him and deny Him access to my inner-most being. I let Him in a bit, but not completely.

I never wanted to lose control. I feared the Holy Spirit's power.

But after praying at the Healing Rooms, the woman said to me, "Have you ever been baptized by the Holy Spirit?"

I'm not going to get into the theology of anything here, except to say that I knew that the Holy Spirit lived within me because by faith I had received the gift of salvation God had given me all those years ago. But I also knew that I had never allowed the Holy Spirit to have full rein in my heart. I had always held something back. I had always felt a check, a nervousness; I had left a guard because I was afraid of letting go, of losing control.

But that day, I knew it was time to say "Yes" to God with no reservations.

So, I told her that I had not been baptized by the Holy Spirit, that I had never spoken in a different tongue, but I wanted to. I wanted to be filled, and I was ready.

She explained that the language I would receive was really a prayer language to be used between me and God—it was a language for prayer, and praise, and supplication. It was a language that would help me express to God all those inexpressible thoughts, and feelings, and requests that we feel so deeply, but cannot express in words. These new words express them, and God understands.

So, I asked God to baptize me and to give me the gift of speaking in tongues.

And then my two prayer partners began to pray in their languages; the woman sang, and it was the most beautiful thing I had ever heard, like some angelic chorus.

I didn't know what to do. I kept saying, "I don't know how." And she kept saying, "You don't have to know how. Just open your mouth."

And then she asked God to remove my fear. To help me give up, let go, open to Him.

And then I felt the wind.

It rushed through my head, and it was hot, like fire.

And I opened my mouth and spoke words I had never spoken before. And somehow I knew that I was speaking right to the heart of God. He heard me and He understood me.

I wept.

We prayed and cried, and prayed and cried for a long time. And when it was done, I felt so quiet and peaceful; exhausted, but at rest. I knew that God had a purpose for me that day, and that's why I had felt such an urge to go to the rooms that day. He wanted me to give myself to Him finally and without reservation.

I've always known that there have been some things in my heart that I haven't been willing to give over to God. Sins that I thought I could keep. Nothing big or horrific, except that they kept me from fully opening to God. So, in that sense, *huge*.

I think I felt that I had given most things to God, and it wouldn't hurt to keep these. I convinced myself that I had tried to give them up, but I just couldn't. I convinced myself that they didn't hurt anyone but me anyway, so they didn't really matter. I said to God, "I can't let go," but what I really meant was, "I *won't* let go. I *won't* give them up. They are mine, and I am going to keep them."

But God has been doing a mighty work in my heart. He is searching me out, trying me, challenging me, cleansing me.

It's funny that when you come to the end of yourself, God is there. And He gently teaches, and asks, and guides, and changes. What I thought I couldn't give up just went without me even fighting anymore. Suddenly the things I was holding onto seemed so insignificant, so stupid in the face of eternity. How could I hold on to *that* thought, or *that* desire instead of God? What could *those* things possibly have for me that God didn't have? How could I continue to say, "I won't!" to the God who suffered and died for me; to the God who said, "I will," for me?

And then I thought of Isaiah 55:

> Come, *all you who are thirsty, come to the waters; and you, who have no money, come buy and eat! Come, buy wine and milk without money and without cost.*
>
> *Why spend money on what is not bread, and your labour on what does not satisfy? Listen, listen to me, and eat what is good, and your soul will delight in the richest of fare.*

I've spent so much of my resources on bread that does not satisfy, and I've filled my minds with thoughts that may delight for a moment, but have no lasting value. And now, here at the end of all things, I begin to see as I've never seen before, that God and God alone satisfies the soul.

Yesterday at church, Stan talked about Romans 12, and what it means to offer our bodies as living sacrifices. The Israelites offered the *whole* animal, not just a part of the animal; the animal was pure and without blemish; and when the sacrifice was complete, the animal was changed.

So, how does that translate to me? It means that I must give myself to God without reservation; I must be whole in body, soul and spirit; whole in mind and heart. I cannot hold anything back, or make excuses, or hold on to something that I think is valuable. I cannot lift my soul to another while I am saying that I am worshipping God. There *is no other!*

That is worship.

And I don't think I ever worshipped God with such a clear single-mindness until that day, in the Healing Rooms, when all my checks and reservations were swept away by the Holy Spirit.

Later, my friend said to me, "Do you think this would have been possible, if you hadn't gotten sick?"

No.

I just would not give myself completely. I would not give up those thoughts. I had convinced myself that I couldn't give them up, and it didn't matter anyway. God had most of me, and that would have to suffice.

It's not the healthy that need a physician; it's the sick and the weak. And it wasn't until my body became so sick and weak that I began to understand the sickness and frailty of my faith.

And it's all very bittersweet. Because what is happening here is what I've been praying for: that God would show me eternity; that He would give me glimpses into the inheritance He has for me; that He would prepare me for my journey. The veil is thinning, and this world's attractions are fading.

Or, maybe, He has a message that He wants me to share: a message of hope, and faith; a message of mercy and reconciliation; a message of renewal; a message of God's purpose for those who love Him.

> Seek the Lord while He may be found; call on Him while He is near. Let the wicked forsake his way and the evil man his thoughts. Let him turn to the Lord, and He will have mercy on him; and to our God, for He will freely pardon.
>
> For my thoughts are not your thoughts, neither are your ways my ways,' declares the Lord. 'As the heavens are higher than the earth, so are my ways higher than your ways, and my thoughts than your thoughts.'

Isaiah 55:6-9

June 15, 2010

Now What?

> *Therefore, since Christ suffered in his body, arm yourself also with the same attitude, because he who has suffered in his body is done with sin.* I Peter 4:11

I read this verse the other day, and I had to go back and read it about seven more times. The phrase that struck me was "he who has suffered in his body is done with sin."

How can anyone be done with sin?

In this state of being refined—day after day, more of the dross being stripped off my soul—I'm left wondering what I'm to do. It's an odd existence. I feel so close to God, so clear-minded, so intent on eternity, so aware that my citizenship is in Heaven.

And then, on the other hand, sometimes so lonely. I'm sort of walking a path that can have no companion except Jesus. No one has been this way and returned. No one is guiding me or walking alongside. All of my friends are willing to go with me, and in their hearts, they *are* walking alongside; *but* they can't really come along; their lives are still pretty firmly planted in the world in which they live.

But I don't really know where I belong anymore. Most of me is still in this world: doing laundry, making lunches, playing with my children, tidying my house; but at the same time, the rest of me is in this new place, a place where making long-term plans seems presumptuous, and where I don't really know what to do with myself. It's a place of transition, maybe.

Part of me wants to forget that I'm sick and go on as before. And maybe that's what I *should* do; maybe I should just continue on as if nothing had happened, and live my life as best I can until I can't anymore or until I'm restored to health.

But that seems so dishonest. So, then I think that maybe I need to prepare in some way for what is to come. The problem is that I don't know *what* is to come, so I don't know what to do. And this is a source of anxiety to me. I like to know what's coming. I like to prepare, and make lists, and check things off, and accomplish things. So, this state of transition is sometimes very stressful. I don't know what to do. I don't know what I *should* be doing. So, I become restless and agitated.

Part of me thinks that I need to be preparing myself for Heaven. But I don't know how to do that.

Another part thinks that I need to prepare myself for pain and suffering. If I am going to get more sick, and eventually die, then, I need to be ready for that—somehow I need to store up my resources and get ready for the long road of suffering to come. If, I am dying, then I probably need to face the fact of long-term hospital time, drug-induced stupors, pain, loneliness … Sigh. I don't know how to do that either. And how ridiculous to think that it's possible to do such a thing. But that's me. I like to be prepared for any eventuality.

And then I need to prepare my children for life without a mother. But I don't know how to do that either—does that mean writing lists? Does that mean shopping for Christmas presents? Does that mean writing a journal of my life? Does that mean composing letters for every major event in their future? I don't know.

So, I came to a point last week, of utter bewilderment.

What do I do?

What *should* I do?

What does God want of me?

How should I then live?

God has brought me so far in the last two months—I've shed

years of bondage to so many things; I've relinquished strong-holds and given up control. I've opened up and let go. And yet, I'm not done with sin.

The sin of thinking that I need to act. The sin of thinking that my future is in my control. The sin of taking over from the God who has all things in His grip. The sin of needing to *do*, and not merely *be*.

Many years ago I worked in the kitchen of a summer camp. One summer, the cook was a very high-stress individual. She was restless and anxious. She worked really hard, and was always striving to keep several steps ahead of the game. I understood why: she was feeding two hundred people three meals a day. It *was* stressful. Add to that ovens that didn't always work, program staff that sometimes ran late, food orders that arrived at mealtimes, and you can see why every day brought challenges that seemed sometimes overwhelming. One day this woman just snapped. The ovens had overheated, and the macaroni was ready 40 minutes early. Program staff couldn't possibly ring the lunch bell so early, especially since the campers were scattered all over the island. In despair, and thinking that this overcooked lunch somehow reflected on her abilities, or her personhood, she just slammed down her wooden spoon and stalked out of the kitchen, never to return.

A few days later, Elvera walked into the kitchen. She had been to camp as a nurse volunteer, but she had never worked as a cook. Ever. And here she was, walking into a strange kitchen and cooking three meals a day for two hundred campers and staff.

She was remarkably cool about it.

I remember on day two, I stood beside her as she stirred a pot of soup on the stove (mouthwatering soup, I'd like to add).

"This is nice," I said.

"Oh, I'm glad you like it," she said, thinking I meant the soup.

"No, not the soup," I explained, "The atmosphere in this kitchen. It's so calm."

"What makes the difference?" she asked.

"There's no striving," I said.

She smiled at that, and then she explained that when she had been praying about this opportunity, she had asked God what to do. She wanted the job, but had no real experience, and while she felt confident she *could* do it, she wanted to know what God thought.

He said to her that she needed to take one day at a time; in fact, that she should take one meal at a time. He told her *not* to prepare *anything* for the next day. He said that each day had enough for itself, and that's what she needed to turn her attention to.

It might be that I've thought of this story because Elvera has been a huge presence in my house lately: she comes for my chemo treatments and stays for the week.

It may be that I've been reflecting on my past, and thinking of all those who have guided and mentored me: she is my Jedi Master in the kitchen and in the things of Jesus.

Or, it may be that this is God's word to me, as I ponder what I should be doing. Maybe God is saying to me that I don't need to do anything for "the future." Maybe I need to do one day at a time. Or, better yet, maybe I need to *be* in one day at a time, and not *do* at all. The desert wanderers gathered enough manna for *one day*; the disciples learned to ask God for *daily* bread. No advanced preparation. No homework. No complicated lists or hoops to jump through. No performance.

Daily bread.

So, what do I do in this season of transition, or how do I live? I received the answer as I read Psalm 27. "One thing I ask of the Lord, this is what I seek; that I may dwell in the house of the

Lord all the days of my life, to gaze upon the beauty of the Lord and seek Him in His temple."

Simple. Just *be*. Find Him where I know He lives and soak in His beauty.

And what will happen when trouble comes? What will happen, if I haven't done any preparation?

> *For in the day of trouble he will keep me safe in his dwelling;*
> *he will hide me in the shelter of his tabernacle and set me*
> *high upon a rock.*

I am already there, where He lives, and so He does the work of saving me. It has *always* been His job to do the saving. Why would it be any different at the end of my life, than it was at the beginning? At the beginning, I didn't even have faith by myself. My faith is a gift from God. My salvation has always come from Him, and it always will.

My role is to wait upon Him. To *be*.

> *I am still confident of this; I will see the goodness of the Lord*
> *in the land of the living. Wait for the Lord; be strong, and*
> *take heart and wait upon the Lord.*

July 5, 2010
A Gift

I went to the last all-school chapel before the summer holidays.

I needed to see the students before they left for the break and to take just a moment to tell them what God has been doing over these five months of my illness, my treatment and their extraordinary prayers.

Because something extraordinary had happened. All around the school.

First, classes throughout the school started taking certain times of the day—different times, so that the whole day was covered; and during that time, no matter what they were doing, the class would stop, and the whole class would take time to pray for me, for my family, for my healing.

Then I heard that in a high school chapel, students had been challenged to step up, to fall on their knees, humble themselves and really get serious with God.

And it happened.

Students went forward for prayer. They wept, and cried out, and repented, and made things right, and asked God what to do—what to do in their own lives, and what to do to help me and my family.

So, the fasting wall was born.

The fasting wall is a bulletin board in the hallway upstairs. The days of the week are listed, and underneath, students anonymously signed up to show that they were fasting and praying on that particular day. They wrote, or left pictures showing how they were fasting, or what they were giving up; for some it is a day of food, for others, their favourite sport, or gaming system, or cell phone, or *all* media.

On the day I saw it, the wall was almost full, but students were still trying to cram their pictures on the wall.

God was moving.

So, on the last all-school chapel, I wanted to go to the students and tell them that God is listening.

I wanted them to know that He is working.

I wanted them to see that I am alive, and to tell them that my heart is being healed, and renewed, and changed, and restored.

And that my body still needs some work.

Mostly, I think I wanted to thank them for their love and to commend them for opening their hearts to God.

I wanted them to know that whatever happens to me, God is still *good*.

I needed to tell them that God is *good* no matter what. Even if my body dies.

And I wanted to tell them how God has helped me through their prayers.

So, I told them about the vision God had given me a few months earlier. I've written about it before. It's the vision of me and my family settled in the palm of God's hand. The hurricane winds are blowing all around, and buffeting the earth, but we are safe and secure, because we are in the centre of His hand, and He has surrounded us with a glass cylinder, like a hurricane glass. We know that we are safe, and we are calling to all our friends and family to join us right there, in the glass, in the centre of His will.

And I told them that God had given us the word *hope*, and that day by day He has been showing us how to access the vast depths of His hope in the midst of sickness and sorrow and hopelessness.

And I said that even when we don't have any answers, if the question starts with God, the answers don't really matter anymore.

And that's all I said. I was pretty choked up by then, and I had promised my children that I would really try not to cry.

The next day, a mother of one of my students came to me and said that she had been in chapel and had heard me speak. She seemed a little teary and overcome. As I looked at her questioningly, she handed me a gift, and her eyes were wide.

"Sandy, I bought this gift for you at the beginning of the week. I was out with the kids, and we popped into this store, and we decided to buy you a gift just to let you know that we love you and we are thinking of you and praying for you every day."

She grabbed my arm, and said, "I bought it *before* that chapel."

I must have looked confused.

"When you open this, you're going to laugh. It's a present from God."

And she said again, "I bought it *before* I heard what you said at chapel, and I didn't really know why I bought it, I just knew I had to buy it for you."

So, I took it home, but forgot to open it until the next morning.

Bryan wasn't home, but Nathan and Anna were, so, I gathered them to me, and asked them to help me open the gift. It was in a big white box, filled with rumpled white tissue. I pulled out the gift, and started to unwrap all the tissue layers.

When I was finished, I held this thing in my hands, and looked at it blankly.

"I don't get it," I said.

"I don't get it either," said Nathan.

"Me neither," said Anna.

"She said it was a present from God," I said.

And then, without knowing why, I began to weep these deep, rending sobs from the depths of my heart. I still wasn't quite sure what I was holding, but I knew it was from God. And then the scales fell from my eyes, and I saw that I was holding a glass cylinder, shaped like a hurricane lamp, and inside was a white feather, still and safe; secure from the buffeting winds all around.

Two days before she heard about it, Lisa walked into a store, and chose—out of all the items in a very extensive gift shop—a physical manifestation of the vision God had given me months earlier.

And just to blow the top off your head a little more:

The white feather.

The feather was not a part of my vision; I saw my family clearly and realistically. However, when I first got the news that the cancer had returned, Nathan and Anna were learning Psalm 91. Almost every night, in his prayers, Nathan would say, "Lord, you said that you will cover us with your feathers, and under your wing we will find refuge. Lord, we need those feathers to cover us now."

The feather is for Nathan and for Anna, because they have hidden His word in their hearts, and because the image of sheltering under the wing of God is so powerful for them.

The feather is God, inside with us, comforting us and keeping us warm.

The poem.

While the feather was not a part of my vision, as soon as I saw it, I thought of a poem by Emily Dickinson. The poem is entitled *Hope Is the Thing with Feathers*.

God gave us the word *hope*.

Here's the poem:

> *Hope is the thing with feathers*
> *That perches in the soul,*
> *And sings the tune—without the words,*
> *And never stops at all,*
> *And sweetest in the gale is heard;*
> *And sore must be the storm*
> *That could abash the little bird*
> *That kept so many warm.*
> *I've heard it in the chillest land,*
> *And on the strangest sea;*
> *Yet, never, in extremity,*
> *It asked a crumb of me.*

God knows about this poem, and He knows that I know about the poem. And He gave it to me to hang in my living room, to remind me that hope is the thing with feathers.

The timing.

On the day I spoke in chapel, I was very weak and tired. I didn't really want to speak. I wasn't sure if I really had anything to say after all. Sometimes it's hard to maintain any faith at all, and my only prayers in the last few days had been, "Lord, I believe; help, Thou, my unbelief."

On that day, I didn't feel that I had any insights to share, or any great words from God. I didn't even really know if I had any hope myself.

God knew that I needed to have my hope renewed. And He did

it in a very personal way, just for me. And this leads me to ...

The method.

People talk about love languages; these are the ways in which we experience love. For some people, words of affirmation are important; for others, it's time together, doing an activity; for others, it's acts of service. For me, because I am obviously a shallow and needy individual, my love language is presents. I love to receive gifts. Gifts of any sort and any size. Surprise gifts, expected gifts, serious gifts and funny gifts. Gifts are my language of love.

And God knows it.

And He chose to affirm my faith, and re-establish my vision, and flood me with His extravagant love with a gift. Wrapped in tissue and tied with a bow.

July 26, 2010

At the Edge of Mount Doom

I've been struggling with the deterioration of my body. Six months ago, I was running twenty kilometres a week, I was fit, and healthy, and strong, and happy. Or, so I thought. Obviously I wasn't as strong and healthy as I thought I was. *But* ... I was so happy with my body, and my fitness, and my strength. I gloried in my ability to run. I felt free. Well. Powerful.

One of my friends had been fretting about how much I was running. She asked why I did it.

"I love it!" I said.

"Why?" she asked.

I thought for a long moment, and then sort of had an epiphany: I didn't really love running. In fact, most of the time I hated it. And it took serious commitment, a certain inflexibility of routine and concerted planning for me to ensure that I did it three times a week. It was always hard, and it always involved a lot of self-talk and encouragement for me to do it. So why did I say so positively, "I love it," when that was patently untrue? Well, I did love how I felt afterwards. I did love the changing strength and fitness of my body. I did glory in the accomplishment of something I had never thought I would do in life.

And I felt powerful.

So after that long moment of thought, I finally said, "I think that if I run, I won't get sick again."

So there you have it: it's all about control. If I do this .... then this will happen. It's all about me, and what I can do with my body.

Obviously, I wasn't conscious of this thought every time I ran, but it certainly became the anthem of my fitness routine. Even more so than the weight loss benefits, flexibility and beauty issues.

I know that fear of aging plagues many people, particularly in the Western world; but I've never really been troubled by the thought. To me, aging is a natural progression of the body and the spirit; it's a sort of rite of passage; a treasure that you discover as you gain the wisdom and serenity of self-discovery and spiritual maturity. And the wrinkles, and kinks, and foibles of the body are outward manifestations of this wisdom.

That's been my philosophy, anyway. Aging didn't seem to be something to be either mourned or feared. I had witnessed my mother age with grace and serenity, always happy to be the age she was, never looking back with regret or forward with fear. Unlike her best friend, who spent the morning of each new birthday locked in the bathroom, sobbing. Each birthday was a cause for celebration for my mom, and I always honoured her for that.

And this was a woman who understood the physical pain of aging. When I say that I was never concerned about growing old, I realize that had I suffered the effects of old age—the often painful deterioration of the body—I might have been singing a different tune. Old age might be something to fear. The complete breakdown of the body and total reliance on others for your physical needs—that might be something to fear. But my mom understood the physical pain of aging. She had suffered debilitating arthritis for years, she had diabetes, and in the end, used a colostomy after a botched surgery. And yet, other than saying that "It's a bugger to get old," she had very few complaints about aging.

So, I've known my whole life that it is possible to age with grace and dignity.

But, facing a terminal illness seems so different than merely growing old. And I guess the difference might be that unlike aging, which is a gradual process, the physical degradation of the body in an illness is steep and precipitous. There is very little time to become accustomed to one major body change before another encroaches upon you. Six months ago, I noticed that my torso was swelling and that I seemed to have gained weight around my middle—but, it wasn't weight gain, it was a liver rapidly growing cancerous tumours.

And then I began chemotherapy. And along with that came all sorts of physical woes. Nausea. Loss of appetite, weight loss, vomiting, diarrhea, fatigue, hair loss. Steroids, prescribed for the nausea, and the liver pain immediately caused swelling of my face and upper torso.

And then the news that that chemo had been useless and ineffective, so a new regime was introduced—one that was even more toxic, and dangerous. Because it is so highly allergenic, I needed much higher doses of the steroid, and the immediate effects on my body were devastating. My face became swollen and moon-like. My cheekbones disappeared and my features blurred. The flesh around my eyes became puffy and distorted. All my hair fell out, and there was nowhere to hide: the classic, steroid-engorged cancer look. My appetite soared, and between that and the steroid puff, I gained twenty pounds. I had no clothes that fit. I bought more, and tried not to look too carefully in the mirror as I tried them on.

All these changes didn't really disturb me at first. In fact, when my appetite returned, and I was able to eat properly again, after those first two devastating rounds of chemo, I rejoiced. I would *much* rather be able to eat anything and everything, that not to be able to eat at all. And that it the truth. So, I was happy, and I celebrated. With food. Lots and lots of food. And I thought to myself that these physical changes were the least of my worries. At that point, three months ago, I really thought I was going to die very soon. I didn't have a lot of hope, because I was so sick. So, a little puffiness and weight gain didn't seem so bad.

But now, two months later, I'm having some issues. Not all the time. But every now and then—like when I catch a glimpse of myself unexpectedly in a mirror. Or when I see someone I haven't seen for awhile, and they kind of do a double take. Or when I am getting dressed, and the swelling for one reason or another is particularly bad that day, and I can't fasten up the larger size I just bought, and I don't think these shorts come in a bigger size. Or when I'm going out and I want to look pretty.

It's not that I was used to being pretty. I've never had a lot of confidence in my outward appearance. I've never been sought after, or admired, or lauded for my beauty. *But*, I was a pretty snappy dresser, and I liked how my style had evolved over the years, and I had come to a place of peace with myself and my looks, after a lifetime of learning to accept myself and my physical foibles. So here I am now, after all these years of hard-fought struggle, and these little tendrils of grief and regret about my appearance are winding themselves around my heart. And I've cried about them. And I've felt like a lesser person.

That's really sad.

It's sad that it has such a hold on me.

It's sad that it took cancer to show me that I still have issues with this one thing I thought I had finally conquered. Because for years, I've been content to be me, and to look like me, no matter the size.

I was talking about this the other day with the same friend who had asked me about my running. I was griping about the puffiness, and the weight gain, and the general blobbiness of my body. She said that she had noticed that looks seemed to be really important to me, and that I seemed to spend a fair amount of time thinking about how I looked, and carefully choosing my wardrobe and accessories. I agreed, because it was all true, and I liked it. I liked dressing well, and putting a look together, and feeling attractive.

And then there was a long pause. And then finally, she said, "Do you think it might be a little bit like your running?"

I looked at her blankly for a moment.

"What do you mean?" I asked.

"Well, you said that your running was all about control. You, trying to control your own health. Do you think this might be all about control, too?"

Another long pause. Another moment of epiphany. Another realization that *control* is the idol I've erected time after time in my life, and that no matter how many times I think I've torn down the Asherah pole, somehow I put it up again and worship at its feet.

Another egotistical deception that needs to be stripped away.

Just when I think that here, exposed on the high places, with nowhere to run or hide, where every possible sin must have been stripped away by now because I feel so exposed and vulnerable, I see that there is more. More layers of gunk that I've built up over the years as a sort of defence against—against what? Against the world? Against public opinion? Against God? Against myself, maybe. If I control how I look, maybe people will like me better, and I won't be lonely, or feel judged, or be teased. I don't know.

The essential me is *not* in toned tummy muscles, and firm thighs, and smooth skin, and sculpted cheekbones. It is not in eternal youth, and good looks, and lovely outfits, and good accessories. It is not in outward appearance. I tell my daughter this every day. I try to model it in my speech. *But* I have failed.

And even as I write this, I feel so shallow. How can this be a source of grief to me in a world like this, where children die of starvation in the streets where I grew up; where refuges swarm to camps already overflowing with desperate, needy, frightened people; where wars ravage the countryside, and people die in ditches; where God is mocked, and babies are killed.

And yet, I do mourn it. And the deception obviously has a hold on my heart.

And so, that's sad.

But, I also know that God knows that I am made of dust. And dust is not very clever.

I feel a little like Frodo Baggins at the end of the world, when he is facing his final test in the fiery furnace of Mount Doom. He knows that he needs to destroy the ring of power; he knows he needs to wrest it off his finger and throw it into the fiery furnace, or Sauron will win and the world will be enslaved in agony and despair.

But he can't do it.

The ring is precious to him. More precious than his freedom. More precious than his friends. More precious than his life. He fears it and worships it. He cannot let it go. It has become part of him, and he feels that to destroy the ring is to destroy himself.

In the end, he never does let it go. He simply cannot do it. He is not the hero who saves Middle Earth. He is the frightened little hobbit who clings to the deception and cannot let it go.

He is made of dust.

In the end, it is Gollum who saves Middle Earth.

Gollum. Hopeless, helpless, morally depraved, sinful.

He didn't mean to save anyone. But when Frodo couldn't, or wouldn't, destroy the ring, Gollum leapt into action. With a single-minded frenzy, he seized Frodo's hand, chewed off his finger, and with a cry of victory and despair, fell into the abyss and was devoured in a sea of lava.

He didn't save the world in any conscious or deliberate way. Like Frodo, he just couldn't let go of his idol, and he preferred to die rather than give it up. At the end of all things, right at the mouth of Hell, He couldn't let go. And he died.

Sometimes I feel that I am standing at the edge of the abyss, looking down into the river of lava at the centre of Mount Doom. It is the end of all things. My feet are torn and dusty, my lips cracked and parched. I am tired, filthy, crabby and confused.

But, I am not alone. And what I've learned more than anything in this journey through the barren places of Mordor is that even though the layers are being stripped away and my soul is exposed and vulnerable, I am in no way diminished. In fact, paradoxically, I am renewed.

Henri Nouwen wrote, "The first step to healing is not a step away from the pain, but a step toward it."

I might be tempted to run away. In fact, I *am* tempted. I've made quite a practice of it in my lifetime. But, this time I don't want to. This time the stakes are too high and eternity looms too near. This time I need to turn and face it; and in facing it, finally be free.

And I am content, because God is with me, and He can do it.

July 31, 2010

Waking Up

I think I've forgotten that a relationship with God is about more than just talking *to* Him and worshipping Him ... It's also about *listening*. Why is it so hard for me to be quiet enough to listen to Him? Even now, it's hard for me to repose myself and be quiet before Him. Other people seem to be hearing from Him on my behalf, but not me.

That's not entirely true. I do think I hear Him through scripture. I think He directs me to verses and speaks clearly through them.

Maybe I just don't have the confidence to state clearly, "This is what the Lord said to me ..."

I wonder if it's linked to what I was talking about in my last blog. Maybe my mind is so filled with these idols I've erected that I am blocked from hearing Him—or maybe just too full of my own stuff to listen.

And even now, I see that the deception has led me to focus once more on appearance and not on what is really happening, which is a fight for my survival—a fight for my healing and the banishment of cancer. I've been so absorbed by the loss of beauty that I haven't been paying attention to the other things happening around me. How is that for sad?

So, the other day, when a friend wrote to me and said that she had a sense of urgency about prayer for me, I was taken aback. Who am I that someone should pray so earnestly for me? And yet, there are literally hundreds of people fasting *and* praying on my behalf. Faithfully, earnestly, *daily*. People I don't even know! It's overwhelming. I don't even think I pray for myself so earnestly. So daily.

In fact, over the last few weeks, I haven't really been praying at all for myself and my healing. I feel as though I've been asleep, or drifting aimlessly. Part of this is because it is summer, and summer tends to be an aimless sort of time; but I think part of it is that I want to forget that I'm sick; I want to play in the sun, and go to the lake, and have dinner with friends, and do all the summertime things I always do without thinking of my body and its disease.

So, I've drifted.

And maybe I've drifted because I've been focussed on the wrong thing.

I remember one summer when Bryan was concerned about two things regarding our house. One was a small leak that had developed on our roof, and the other was the need to paint some of the rooms inside. So, one concern was functional and one was cosmetic. Needless to say, I convinced Bryan, against his better judgement, that painting the rooms, and making them pretty was *much* more important than fixing the roof. Appearance was more important than function.

I focussed on the wrong thing. That winter the leak grew, and by the next summer, we had to replace the entire roof, rather than patch just a corner.

So when I say that I've been asleep, I wonder if my aimlessness is due to this idol I've been talking about; I can't see reality clearly because my eyes and sensibilities are so clouded. Or, maybe it's been a deliberate closing of my eyes to truths or questions I haven't wanted to face.

When people ask me how I am, I always say, "I'm okay," or "Well, we're taking one day at a time," or something suitably vague like that. Because the truth is that I don't really know how I am. I don't know if the chemo is working, I don't know if the cancer is shrinking, I don't even know most of the time how I am feeling because so much of how I'm feeling is because of chemo, or the drugs—so it's difficult to say what part of my discomfort is because of chemo, and what part is because of cancer, and what part is because of being tired of it all and wanting some reprieve.

So, I don't know how I'm doing.

And I think I might have convinced myself that I don't really care. I think maybe I made an almost unconscious decision to suspend those kinds of questions until summer was over. Certainly, I didn't want to think about them on Hornby Island. I didn't want to be ill or to discuss my illness on the island; I just wanted a holiday. I had one day when I felt very fatigued and ill. I couldn't explain how I felt, and I didn't want to embrace it—I wanted to ignore it, and I resented my body for having the effrontery to let the cancer have a part of my time with the Robinsons on our island. Part of the problem was that when I feel like that, my brain is very foggy, and I feel isolated and alone, and I can't articulate my thoughts. So, while I wanted to let people in, I couldn't do it, and the day ended up as a disaster for me (and for anyone else who figured out what was going on).

But, for the most part, we were pretty successful in putting cancer away.

And then we came back. And I had to have chemo two days later, when we were still basking a little bit in the afterglow of holiday time.

I cried when I walked into the hospital.

Two days later, Anna had a breakdown (more about that in a blog to come).

As a result, Bryan had a breakdown while on the phone with Laurie.

A week of sleeplessness made Laurie hyper-sensitive, and she had a breakdown.

It was a bit of a disaster all around.

For me, it wasn't really worse than usual, except for the fact that it was so difficult for everyone else in my family. The beginning was hard, but apart from that, things went about the same for me. What *was* hard was that Bryan, Anna and Laurie were struggling so much, and I was completely unable to engage in their struggle, *or* do anything to help them. The chemo makes me disengage with my emotions, and makes me very foggy and unaware of others. So, when I came to my real senses a few days later, and realized what had happened in my absence, I felt that I had abandoned my family.

And then things started happening. People started asking questions about my treatment and my future; about decisions they thought I needed to be making; people began e-mailing me, telling me about visions they had seen and dreams they had experienced. Before I knew it, my doctor was calling, and asking me to make decisions, and giving me choices I wasn't ready to make.

I was confused.

And a little angry.

The whole point was that I didn't *want* to make any choices. Not in the summer. Not when the sun was shining. Not when I didn't know where those choices would lead. I didn't *want* to know. I wanted to pretend that it was summer as usual at the Glum home.

But, as I read more e-mails, and talked more rationally with the people around me, I realized that God was working and that if I wasn't careful, I would miss what was going on. Other people were clearly hearing from God on my behalf, and I had better listen.

And that's when I realized that I been out to lunch for a few weeks. God had been moving, but I hadn't noticed.

A couple of weekends ago, several people had dreams and visions and upset sleep patterns all focussed on me. One friend had a vision of the cancer in my body; she took it and squeezed it; over the course of several days, she continued to squeeze it until there was nothing left but a dry, white stone; she crumbled that to dust, and then she plunged her hands into a cleansing stream while reciting verses of healing that the Lord had shown her. Another friend saw my liver, and there was a demon on top; he asked the Lord if there was a demon of cancer; when the Lord said, "Yes," my friend said, "Well, that demon has no business in Sandy Glum," and he cast it out; he says that out of the corner of his eye, he saw it leave. Another friend hasn't slept for weeks, and we think, now, that her sleeplessness may have been due to some spiritual warfare that had been happening around our families. Many people have written to me with verses about healing, and several people have said that they feel a sense of urgency, that God is ready to move. Many had verses that God had given them over the week, and some of the verses coincided with verses that God had given me throughout the week.

I began to listen to God.

So, today, I have some ladies coming by to pray for me; and tonight I have some high school students coming to pray. These kids have been reading about healing miracles, and have been praying for me for months; and so when they called and said that they had a burden to pray for me, and a real sense that they need to come over and pray for a miracle, I told them that they should come soon; that God was working; and that others were feeling the same. A sense of urgency.

So, I am excited and apprehensive. In typical Sandy fashion, I feel a little ashamed that I didn't begin this; that I wasn't the one who heard from God first, or rather, that I wasn't the one listening to God; that I was looking somewhere else, and I was focussed on something irrelevant while God was working; that I wasn't in the loop until the loop had finished.

That I wasn't in control.

But, I think I'm over that now.

I'm awake again.

I'm praying again.

I'm awaiting God.

And I'm expecting Him to move ...

August 2, 2010

The Family Tree

A few things have shaken me up recently, and my mind is full of so many thoughts. It's hard to sort through them all, and figure out what it all means, and what I should be doing about it, or thinking about it; what I need to dwell on, and what I need to let go.

We have a big, beautiful maple tree in our front yard. It's a vine maple, with huge leaves. Every autumn, we rake the leaves, make huge piles, and dive into their crispy depths. We love the tree.

When Bryan's brother comes to visit, part of the tradition is that he takes a family picture in front of this tree. He has been doing it since his son Matthew, now 18, was an infant. And we laugh about it because he always does it on the last day, minutes before he leaves, so it's always a rush, and people are always a little crabby about it (mostly me) and Bruce gets really flustered and funny. It has become a lovely family tradition, and we have eighteen years of beautiful photos depicting the growth of the tree and our families.

Sadly, our tree has been gradually dying. This summer it didn't produce very many leaves, and we decided that it was time to have someone look at it. Bryan called in someone who knows about trees, and he confirmed our fears: the tree was sick and needed to be cut down. Enormous limbs were dry and brittle, and he feared that if we didn't remove the tree that it would pose a danger in the winter months when around here the wind blows six days out of seven. Really blows.

So, we talked to some people, and made some more calls, and booked someone to come and remove the tree. Remove it. From top to bottom. And then drill out the trunk. Until the only thing left would be piles of sawdust.

And we looked around, and decided that since they were taking out that tree, they may as well take out some other trees that had grown too big and were now looming over the house, dropping cones, and needles, and branches on our roof; the roof that we are replacing in a couple of weeks.

It made sense to us.

But then we made a really big mistake.

We discussed our plans with everyone who came over. That's just what Bryan does; he is an oral learner, and it helps him process information if he can discuss it. Plus he is naturally very chatty, and he likes to get other people's input.

We didn't notice that at each retelling of the photos tradition, Anna became more and more intrigued with the tree. She asked if there were pictures of her near the tree. She remembered that it was one of the first trees she had ever climbed, and she noticed that the Robinsons were also cutting down some of her climbing trees. She has always been uber-interested in sickness and disease, and she obsessed about the tree.

"Daddy, what is wrong with the tree?"

"It's sick, Anna."

"But what *kind* of sickness does it have, Daddy?"

"I don't know, Anna—just a sickness that trees get. *You* can't get sick from the tree." (Lots of reassurance on this, because she always thinks that she will be infected by someone else.)

"I know that, Daddy." (Very scornfully.) "But why can't the tree get better? People get better when they're sick, right?"

**Yes. We should have had red flags flying high by now. Yes. We should have realized that this wasn't really about the tree any more. Yes. We should have reined in our own talk about the tree, and how sad we were about cutting it down.

But we didn't.

I had just had a treatment.

It was the first summertime treatment, when the kids couldn't escape to school and leave the sickness behind.

It was the first treatment without Elvera who makes them laugh.

It was the first treatment where Bryan was alone in the house with a sick wife and two frightened children. (Albeit, children who for the most part, manage these fears very well.)

Our defences were down.

So, the day came for the tree cutters to begin. They were going to do the maple tree first, and then move on to the fir trees.

It was day three after treatment, and I was in bed with a very foggy head and no energy. In fact, I hardly noticed the noise, and I certainly couldn't muster up any emotion. Disengaged— one of the worst side-effects of chemo; especially when you have an emotionally needy seven-year-old.

The saw began to cut, and Anna began to weep. And wail. And dissolve into a heap of hysterical seven-year-old on the floor.

Bryan came into my room, white-faced. "We've made a terrible mistake," he gasped. "I think we should make them stop."

I gazed at him blankly; unable to process his words. Finally I grasped the meaning. "No! We've done all the discussion, and we need to cut down the tree. I don't want to have to go through all this again. Why are you trying to make me think today? I can't think today. I can't make any decisions today. Go away!"

Nice.

So, Bryan phoned Laurie, and burst into tears on the phone. He had just had enough. And neither of us had ever really done any crying over this round of cancer. We hadn't had time. Once we returned from Spring Break, we were launched into this crazy rollercoaster ride of hideous CT results, and toxic treatment, and hospital visits, and more. Bryan hadn't had time to do his customary talk-through and processing. So he was just done. Even more so than Anna.

So, he sobbed.

And then Laurie sobbed.

And then, in typical Laurie fashion, she found some help.

Gord showed up ten minutes later with Timmy's coffee and doughnuts. And they walked around the yard and talked about the projects Bryan had planned.

I'm not sure when in the timeline he called a halt to the cutting, but when I came to my senses a few days later, I realized that the maple tree was still standing in the front yard. The top was gone, but the bottom was still there: the photo part, the climbing part.

"Hey, what's up with the tree?" I said.

He looked at me sheepishly, and said, "I just couldn't do it."

And Anna came up and wound herself around me and said, "Daddy saved our tree, Mummy. He says that trees don't recuperate when they are sick, but I think trees can recuperate, don't you, Mummy? Because if people can recuperate, then trees can recuperate, right?"

And in a blinding flash I saw that this had never really been about the tree at all; it was about me. And cancer. And a little girl who needs to believe that things get better when they are sick; a little girl who needs us to hope against hope; a little girl who needs us to choose life.

I looked over at Bryan, who still looked a bit sheepish. "Wow. You made the right choice. How did you do it, when everything was falling apart at the seams?"

He said, "I couldn't break my baby's heart."

So that tree is now standing topless in the sunny patch of our front yard. It is more than a testimony of family, and growth, and good times. To me, it is a symbol of a father's love for his child. I try to imagine sometimes, in my lesser moments, the expressions on the guys' faces when this deranged father came stumbling out of the house calling, "*Stop! Stop!*" And explaining that he had changed his mind. It makes me laugh a little ... and cry a little. Because I know that what people thought of him would never be a consideration that Bryan would entertain.

A symbol of a father's love for his daughter. His desire to care for her heart; to protect, and nurture, and hold her safe.

A symbol of hope. Maybe the tree (having been refined not by fire, but by saw) might sprout some new branches next year.

Like me.

Later, we were talking as a family, and everyone was catching me up with what had happened while I was away on chemo. And for awhile, it was all about Anna and how she had suffered over the week with her many griefs.

But finally Nathan spoke up. We had never heard what he thought about the tree. He had never said anything.

But now he said to his sister, "Anna, a tree is like a person. If one person in your family is sick and won't get better, you have to look around and find another one to help take its place. You should have looked for another tree."

Knife to the heart.

Twist.

I looked at this profound little man, comprehension dawning on my face. All summer long, I had noticed that Nathan had begun to be very affectionate to the women in our life. Lots of hugs and snuggles. He has never been a snuggler with anyone but me—not even with Laurie. But suddenly he was snuggling everyone: Laurie, Elvera, Shannon, his aunties. Like he was looking around to see who might be able to give him the snuggles when he needed them; to see who could take the place of a mummy who has to leave.

My heart is going to break.

On the one hand, I'm appalled that my ten-year-old has such thoughts in his head; and on the other hand, I'm proud and happy to think that he is so mature, so profound, so aware of reality. I'm thankful that he has clear vision, and that he is taking the initiative to form relationships that are going to be crucial to him in his future.

But it is one of those things that has shaken me up. A couple of days ago, I wrote about *my* dream for the summer: to forget.

But events *and* people (mostly unintentionally) have conspired against me and have forced me to remember.

And *that* has shaken me up, too.

Because there must be a reason why.

And I hate not knowing.

But now again, I'll have to suck it up, and take it to God, and place it once again in His hands.

Along with my tree, and my husband, and my children, and my friends.

And I'll retreat once again to my hurricane lamp where we can rest secure in the palm of God's hand.

It's a good place to be, even in the summer.

Afterword

Darling Sandy died on September 24, 2010. It wasn't what she and her friends had expected. Through prayer and scripture, they had faith that she would be physically healed—that she would live a *long life*. Between September 2008 and February 2010 she was "blog-silent." This period had been her time of respite from cancer treatments and tests—a time of relative peace and hope, hope that she had indeed been physically "healed."

But throughout August and into September of 2010, Sandy, her family, and her medical team were confounded by the rapid regrowth of the cancer in her liver and lymph nodes, despite the steady infusions of chemo and radiation that were still being inflicted on her tired, battle-worn body. As the battle raged, she confessed privately to a friend that she had been experiencing increased weakness, pain, and discomfort—but she wasn't admitting it to those closest to her. She was looking out for others to the end.

A final radiation treatment at the end of August took her and Laurie to Victoria one final time. It was a precious and peaceful time of enjoying walks and good food, a movie (*Eat, Pray, Love*), prayer, scripture reading, hugs, and of course, tears. They had a sense that something serious, sobering, was on the horizon but they didn't dare put it into words. Their hearts couldn't manage to embrace it.

Sandy returned home for Nathan's birthday. "I can remember anxiously waiting to greet him eleven years ago. Life happens too quickly ... And then you are here (sigh)."

The toxic blend of weakness, pain, and pain meds increased throughout September. And then suddenly, one day mid-month, the pain and the meds decreased, and she seemed to be miraculously rallying. Everyone thought so. Was this perhaps the "healing" they had hoped for?

She planned burgers and beer for her dad and Bryan while they watched the football game—thrilled being back to the "normal"-ness of life.

But it was short-lived.

By the next day she was too weak to be left alone. By the day after that, Laurie had moved in to assist Bryan with the enormous demands—emotional and practical—that her care placed on him.

"Do you think I'm dying?" she had asked Laurie.

"I don't know, but I think so ..." Laurie had responded, the reality now squeezing her heart.

Bryan and Laurie sat down with Nathan and Anna the following day, to let them know that their mom might die. The next day, her final one, she had simply sat on the edge of her bed in the early morning and declared, "I have to go now ... I have to go now." She lay back down on her bed and swiftly descended into a coma.

By the time she arrived at the hospital (she had made it clear that she did not want to die at home—she didn't want that memory for her kids) there was little to be done. She died a mere 2 1/2 hours after being admitted.

Friends and family had believed in the possibility of her complete physical healing to the heart-rending end. Some even prayed over her lifeless body at the funeral home, hoping that the healing might manifest itself in a resurrection. To no avail. It was finished. Our beauty was gone.

CPSIA information can be obtained
at www.ICGtesting.com
Printed in the USA
FSOW02n1825190215
5306FS

9 780993 703041